The IMF, The World Bank, Humanitarian Organisations and Development

Felicien Dago

Published by New Generation Publishing in 2021

Copyright © Felicien Dago 2021

First Edition

The author asserts the moral right under the Copyright, Designs and Patents Act 1988 to be identified as the author of this work.

All Rights reserved. No part of this publication may be reproduced, stored in a retrieval system or transmitted, in any form or by any means without the prior consent of the author, nor be otherwise circulated in any form of binding or cover other than that which it is published and without a similar condition being imposed on the subsequent purchaser.

ISBN   978-1-80369-145-9

www.newgeneration-publishing.com

New Generation Publishing

By the same author

Politics, Economics and Development in Sub-Saharan Africa

The right to development is an inalienable human right.

- UN General Assembly Resolution 41/128 of 4 December 1986

Development has to be woven around people, not people around development.
It has to be development of the people, by the people and for the people.

- Nayak (2008:2)

Human development is an ongoing journey, not a destination. Its centre of gravity has always been about more than just meeting basic needs. It is about empowering people to identify and pursue their own paths for a meaningful life, one anchored in expanding freedoms.

- UNDP (2020:6), The 2020 Human Development Report

CONTENTS

EXECUTIVE SUMMARY 2

1. INTRODUCTION 5

2. LITERATURE REVIEW 7
2.1 DEVELOPMENT.. 7
2.2 THE BRETTON WOODS INSTITUTIONS...................... 13
2.2.1 THE CRISES 21
2.2.2 REFORM AND STATUS QUO 30
2.3 HUMANITARIAN ORGANISATIONS 34
2.3.1 DEVELOPMENT AS CONNECTIVITY AND MORE 35
2.3.2 CONTINUOUS INCREMENTAL IMPROVEMENT....... 48
2.4 SUMMARY 54

3. METHODS... 65
3.1 SURVEY 65
3.2 RESULTS 69

4. DISCUSSIONS 77
4.1. FINDINGS... 77
4.2. LIMITATIONS 83

5. CONCLUSIONS... 87

6. RECOMMENDATIONS.. 94

REFERENCES 98

APPENDICES.. 135

All Praises and Thanks to GOD Almighty. In Heaven.

Infinite Gratitude to Mum and Dad; and to my best friends Christine, Briella and Samuell.

As well as to my Guardians and Protectors: Manmie, Georgette, Marthe, Yao, Camille and Amlan.

Dr. Felicien Dago is an educator with decades of experience teaching Spanish, French, Business as well as Information and Communication Technology (ICT) in schools in and around London; and online. Over recent years, he has taught English as a Second Language and English for Academic Purposes; and ICT in the Middle East.

Felicien has travelled extensively in order to meet other cultures and new people.

He enjoys doing research; learning enriching things and subjects. He is passionate about progress, current affairs, education, history, communication technology, economic development, international relations and so on.

His hobbies include driving, cooking, gardening, reading, working out and spending time with friends and family.

Dr. Dago holds various qualifications including a B.Sc. (Hons) in Information Systems, an MBA, a DBA, a QTS, a Master in International Cooperation and Humanitarian Aid, a CELTA, a TESOL Diploma, and an MA in TESOL. He strives to learn as much as possible about humanitarian organisations and their input in human and economic development around the globe.

Executive Summary

Development seems to have almost always been a preoccupation and a priority; at least if moments like the creation of the Bretton Woods institutions, the Marshall Plan, the Millennium Development Goals (MDGs), Sustainable Development Goals (SDGs) and Agenda 2030 - to name but a few – are anything to go by.

The International Bank for Reconstruction and Development (IBRD), also known as the World Bank, one of the Bretton Woods institutions; was tasked with development. It works in close collaboration with the International Monetary Fund (IMF) which 'promotes international financial stability and monetary cooperation; facilitates international trade, promotes employment and sustainable economic growth, and helps to reduce global poverty' (IMF, 2021).

Their combined actions in favour of development all over the world is being studied in this paper.

The development actions of humanitarian organisations – primarily devoted to saving lives and relieving human suffering – are also being examined. This comparative analysis relies on the literature as well as the results of a survey, which participants are from all walks of life and from a wide range of backgrounds and professions.

The World Bank, the IMF and the humanitarian organisations have been in operation for decades; probably a testament to their necessary, relevant and highly needed input and contributions to humankind.

Both types of organisations therefore, taken individually, must have good practices that can advance the cause of and contribute to development all over the world.

For the purpose of the present study, a survey is being conducted in relation to which group of organisations: the Bretton Woods institutions or the humanitarian organisations is better equipped to foster and deliver development around the globe.

The survey results appear to align, for most part, with the literature.

1. INTRODUCTION

In the existence of living organisms and countries, *development* is most probably unavoidable, inescapable and a must.

For people and countries, various organisations are set up worldwide to (help) deliver that development.

This study will dwell on humanitarian organisations and the Bretton Woods institutions: the World Bank and the International Monetary Fund (IMF).

In the specific case of human beings, their surroundings, environment and countries, what is *development*? Can it be measured?

If yes, how?

If not, why not?

In their respective spheres of activity and influence, how do humanitarian organisations and the Bretton Woods institutions approach *development*?

What have their contributions been like? What actual form(s) do those contributions take? How are their respective results and track records? Which type of organisations will the survey in the present study reveal as best suited for development?

In view of the critical importance of development in an increasingly environmentally focused world, the World Commission on Environment and Development (WCED) published the Brundtland Report about "sustainable development [which] requires meeting the basic needs of all and extending to all the opportunity to fulfil their aspirations for a better life" (WCED, 1987). Theoretically, development will remain a component of human needs and realities.

2. LITERATURE REVIEW

Which type of organisations is or has been performing better to deliver *development*?

Answering this question will require a thorough understanding of *development* and the two types of organisations being analysed: the *Bretton Woods institutions* and *humanitarian organisations* which actions and approach to development this study is scrutinising.

2.1 Development

> ...there is no single blueprint for development.
> - Noor (2015:94)

This paper which revolves around development, humanitarian organisations and the Bretton Woods institutions has at its core human beings, nations and countries.

Human beings create, embody nations and countries.

It is an obvious fact that the World Bank, the International Monetary Fund (IMF) and humanitarian organisations exist and work for human beings: inhabitants of countries and nations. In other words; these organisations' goal, their objective, their purpose, their beneficiary, their consumer and their customer is ultimately the human being.

There is no development but for people; and but for human beings.

In the words of Nayak (2008:2): "People must be at the center of human development. Development has to be woven around people, not people around development.

It has to be development of the people, by the people and for the people."

Along similar lines, Rahman, Raja and Conor (2020:2) assert that "The ultimate purpose of economic growth is to provide a better quality of life to the people".

To township, slum, and favela dwellers; to people onboard a Zodiac inflatable boat across the Mediterranean Sea, heading North, in search of a brighter tomorrow; development is not what Amoaka (1998; in Mkandawire and Soludo, 1998:viii), Thomas (2004:1), Karpowicz (2008:1) and Ngirumpatse (2019) respectively make it out to be: "a complex process"; something "contested, ... complex, and ambiguous"; "a catch-all phrase" or an entity "with diverse and competing views".

Development is rather simple. It looks like London, Madrid, Paris, Tokyo, New York and so on. Development looks like a Cambridge, Oxford, Harvard, Princeton education, and so on. Development looks like a Mercedes Benz, a BMW, a Porsche, a Range Rover, a Rolls Royce and so on. It feels like Prada, Versace, Hermès, Dior, Balenciaga, Louis Vuitton, Burberry and so on. Development is a pleasant, comfortable, affluent, happy life; with food on the table, money in the bank, a roof over one's head, healthy-clothed-well educated children and so on. Development is the opportunity; the pathway which leads to the greatest things in life and the ability to live worry-free; at least in relation to everyday *necessities*.

Duffy (2002:253) attests that "we all have an intuitive understanding of the term development".
    Corroborates Qureshi (2019:381): "The term Development is used to describe improvements in the lives of people."
    Moreover, UNDP (2020:6) adds that human development is "more than just meeting basic needs. It is about empowering people to identify and pursue their own paths for a meaningful life, one anchored in expanding freedoms".

The takes that Amoaka (1998), Thomas (2004:1), Karpowicz (2008:1) and Ngirumpatse (2019) have of development appear too intellectual, 'Ivory Tower'-like, philosophical and theoretical. These perceptions and views appear to stem from affluent people from a rich; already *developed* country.

When living on $1 or less a day; development could simply mean the next meal.

Development, as described by Hausmann, Rodrik and Velasco (2008:324):

"the raising of human capabilities in general [through] Higher levels of living standards [that] are the most direct route to achieving improvements in social and human indicators" is the type of development that this work relates to, focuses on and aspires to.

Wherever one is; whatever perspective one takes it from; d*evelopment* implies and entails *growth*. The Oxford dictionary states:

- **Growth:**

a. "the process in people, animals or plants of growing physically, mentally or emotionally"
b. "an increase in the size, amount or degree of something"

- **Development:**

c. "the steady growth of something so that it becomes more advanced, stronger, etc."
d. "*(economics)* the growth of the economy of a country or region through increased business activity"
e. "the process of producing or creating something new or more advanced; a new or advanced product or idea".

Development and *growth* are closely interrelated, interconnected; so much so that they could sometimes be used complementarily and interchangeably.

For Karpowicz (2008:1, 2, 3): 'growth and development are, actually, two different phenomena. Economic growth is but one of many elements the notion of development comprises. Growth does not equal development.

Growth is quantity, development is quality'.

To Duffy (2002:253), "development is synonymous with economic growth".

Rahman, Raja and Conor (2020:3) agree when they write that: "Economic growth is essential for a persistent overall development of a country."

Similarly, Karpowicz (2008:1) sees growth as a precondition to development.

Although this study focuses on development and definitions **b, c, d, e** above; its objective and end-consumer is the human being; hence definition **a:**

- "the process in people (…) of growing physically, mentally or emotionally".

From definition **c**, one could retain the phrase "the steady growth"; sign of constant, perpetual, continuous increase and expansion.

Sums up World Bank (2005:81): "The challenge of development is to transform growth episodes into sustained growth."

Development "can be defined as bringing about social change that allows people to achieve their human potential. (…) Another important point is that development is a **process** rather than an outcome: it is dynamic in that it involves a change from one state or condition to another.

Ideally, such a change is a positive one - an improvement of some sort (for instance, an improvement in maternal health). Furthermore, development is often regarded as something that is done by one group (such as a development agency) to another (such as rural farmers in a developing country). Again, this demonstrates that development is a political process, because it raises questions about who has the power to do what to whom." (SOAS, Unknown a) [Emphasis added]

In this respect, various actors or initiators come the mind such as the local or national authorities and governments; as well as the Bretton Woods institutions and humanitarian organisations.

Development is neither a spontaneous generation nor a new reality (SOAS, Unknown b). Therefore, and potentially, as long as there will be human beings; there shall be development.

From its inception, development which draws its required resources from nature appears to have been negatively impacting the environment (SOAS, Unknown a). At least, until the Brundtland Report. It introduced the concept of *sustainable development*: "meeting the basic needs of all and extending to all the opportunity to fulfil their aspirations for a better life" (WCED, 1987).

In other words meeting present generations' needs without endangering the planet and jeopardising the livelihood and the existence of future generations.

Indeed, "Development is a process that creates growth, progress, positive change or the addition of physical, economic, environmental, social and demographic components.

The purpose of development is a rise in the level and quality of life of the population, and the creation or expansion of local regional income and employment opportunities, without damaging the resources of the environment. Development is visible and useful, not necessarily immediately, and includes an aspect of quality change and the creation of conditions for a continuation of that change." (SID, 2021)

Therefore, in 2015, the United Nations (UN) states members adopted the 2030 Agenda for Sustainable Development which revolves around 17 Sustainable Development Goals (SDGs). (SDGS, Unknown) (Appendix B).

Development is for people as it is for countries.
    It is measured in a wide range of ways. For instance:
- Gross Domestic Product (GDP),
- Gross National Product (GNP),
- GNP per capita,
- Births and death rates,
- Human Development Index (HDI),
- Gender Development Index (GDI),
- Infant mortality rate,
- Gender Empowerment Measure (GEM),
- Human Freedom Index (HFI), (CATO Institute)
- Literacy rate,
- Index of Economic Freedom, (The Heritage Foundation)
- Life expectancy, (Tutor2u, 2021)
- Access to safe water,
- People per doctor, (BBC, 2021)
- Inequality-adjusted HDI, (IHDI)
- Multidimensional Poverty Index, (MPI)
- Genuine Progress Indicator (GPI), (Study Rocket, Unknown; Heikkinen, 2021:16)
- Gross National Happiness, (GNH)
- Happy Planet Index, (HPI)
- Greenhouse Developmental Rights, (GDR) (Heikkinen, 2021:22-29)
- Economic structure,
- Aid received (RGS, Unknown).

All these indicators and measures can be divided into two groups:
- **economic indicators**; for example; GDP, GNP, economic structure, aid received;
- and **social indicators**; such as literacy rate, life expectancy, people per doctor (RGS, Unknown); "nutrition, housing, income distribution, as well as other aspect of cultural and social development." (Hicks and Streeten, 1979:570)

An indicator such the Human Development Index (HDI) was created and is calculated by the United Nations Development Program (UNDP). "It measures average life expectancy, level of education and income for each country in the world" (BBC, 2021).

The UN, through its various organisations and specialised agencies, work on delivering development. The Bretton Woods institutions: the World Bank and the International Monetary Fund (IMF) are two such specialised agencies.

2.2 The Bretton Woods institutions

Errare humanum est, perseverare autem diabolicum.

Avoiding the recurrence of all the conditions which led to the 1930s Great Depression (You, 2002:1); dealing with the devastations of the Second World War and the imminence of reconstruction in the aftermath of the conflict prompted the creation in July 1944 of the International Monetary Fund (IMF) and the World Bank.

The latter institution comprises the International Bank for Reconstruction and Development (IBRD) and the International Development Association (IDA). Development seems to have always been the principal raison d'être of the World Bank. Indeed, from its inception; it was destined to "serve to improve the capacity of countries to trade by lending money to war-ravaged and impoverished countries for reconstruction and development projects."

(Bretton Woods Project, 2019) or (Driscoll, 1996; Kayira and Hope, 1997:118; Brown, 2001:134; Akyuz, 2015:476; Helleiner, 2015:48; Kwagyang, Ghide and Haruna, 2015:51; Frieden, 2017:13).

The World Bank is even often referred to as a ***development agency*** (James, 1996:136; UNHCR, 2020:11), a "multilateral **development** bank" (Ruger, 2005:61); an "international **development** agency [with] expertise for **development**" (Akyuz, 2015:476); and also as a ***development bank*** (Keeley, 2012:56; Staicu and Barbulescu, 2017).

Masters and Chatzky (2019) called the World Bank "the preeminent international institution for **economic development and poverty reduction**". [Emphasis added]

Citing Kapur, Lewis and Webb (1997:168); Ruger (2005:60) also wrote of the World Bank being "the "world's premier economic multilateral" institution".

The IBRD and IDA, together with the
- International Finance Corporation (IFC),
- Multilateral Investment Guarantee Agency (MIGA) and the
- International Centre for Settlement of Investment Disputes (ICSID)

form the World Bank Group (You, 2002:4; World Bank Group, 2021a).

"The World Bank Group works with developing countries to reduce poverty and increase shared prosperity, [it] provides financing, policy advice, and technical assistance to governments, and also focuses on strengthening the private sector in developing countries." (World Bank Group, 2021b) or (Masters and Chatzky, 2019)

The mission attributed to the IMF in July 1944 was to "create a stable climate for international trade by harmonising its members' monetary policies, and maintaining exchange stability [and] to provide temporary financial assistance to countries encountering difficulties with their balance of payments." (Bretton Woods Project, 2019).

The IMF "acts as a monitor of the world's currencies." (World Bank Group, 2021b).

It "is primarily a monetary and not a development institution" (James, 1996:618); and as such was deemed 'at a comparative disadvantage in the areas of poverty and economic growth'. (Bird, 2001:830)

Each year, the World Bank and the International Monetary Fund (IMF) respectively publish:
- the World Development Report: an analysis of economic development aspects (World Bank Group, 2021c) and
- the World Economic Outlook Report: analysis and forecast of member countries' economic developments and policies (IMF, 2021).

The World Bank and the IMF have progressively been working in a tandem
(Reisman, 1992:S349-S350, S387; Dominguez, 1993:368; Driscoll, 1996; Kayira and Hope, 1997:118; Lancaster, 1997:181; Brown, 2001:139; Colgan, 2002; Irish Times, 2002; You, 2002:10; Lombardi and Bessma 2010:16; Willis, 2011:63; Wolff, 2013:86-87, 112; Yakubovska, 2013:72; NBB, 2014; Thibane and Wait, 2017:7; Vreeland, 2019:210).

James (1996:144) and Daste (2015:29) respectively write about "overlap" and "overlaps and conflicts of jurisdiction" between those two Bretton Woods institutions.

"The role of the IBRD is more active and visible while the involvement of the IMF is indirect, through its involvement in the financing procedures of the WB." (Voutsa, Borovas and Fotopoulos, 2014:83) or (Kwagyang, Ghide and Haruna, 2015:51).

This study will observe their unity of action, in relation to development. In that respect, and as a whole; the World Bank and the IMF seem to have been facing several challenges in upholding their 1944 founding aims and mandates.

"The quarter century following the creation of the Bretton Woods institutions saw the greatest prosperity in human history around the world except in much of Africa and parts of Asia and is deservedly dubbed the Golden Age." (You, 2002:4)

It could be argued that the 1970s Oils Shocks ushered in a new era (Dominguez, 1993:369). The response and strategy from the Bretton Woods institutions was the Washington Consensus in the 1980s: "an approach to development born out of the integration of the traditional IMF concerns for macroeconomic stability (anti-inflation, anti-deficit policies) and the Bank agenda of efficiency enhancing reforms (openness, competition, deregulation, privatization)." (You, 2002:10) or (Colgan, 2002)

The Structural Adjustment Programs (SAPs), key to the Washington Consensus; as subsequently evaluated by the Bretton Woods' own analysts found "no systematic effects on growth, inflation and income distribution" (You, 2002:11); a fact also observed by Lahdenperä and Humayoun (2010:25), Moghalu (2019:244) and Cepeda (2021).

Even the World Bank (2005:276) acknowledges that "the stronger macroeconomic policies of the 1980s had not achieved more rapid progress in development and poverty reduction".

The consequences were still drastic falling living standards, for instance in Sub-Saharan Africa (Colgan, 2002; You, 2002:14) and the former Soviet Union (You, 2002:13).

Quoting a research by Khan, Nsouli and Wong (2002); Lahdenperä and Humayoun (2010:25) explain that economies not subjected to the structural adjustment fared better than those that were. That remark is also made by Bustanul (2017:119).

"The IMF and the World Bank's own evaluations of SAPs revealed that the programs failed due to their emphasis on short-term stabilization rather than long-term economic development and poverty reduction." (Noor, 2015:85)

On a related matter, although the World Bank Group had been investing heavily in education worldwide by 2011; for instance, the loan conditionalities imposed on Kenya by the IMF restricted the expansion of education.

Stiglitz (2001) wrote of "paying lip service to education, especially of girls". Probably, due to the fact that "Traditional theories of development may have overlooked education as a stimulus for development" (Duffy, 2002:258).

Cited by Heldt (2018:570); 'Weaver (2008) analyzes the **organized hypocrisy** of the World Bank, meaning **the gap between claimed standards and goals and actual policies**.' [Emphasis added]

In *Chapter Six* (pages 176 – 192) aptly titled *The Fog of Development*; Weaver (2008) explains: "The Hypocrisy of the World Bank has been present throughout the institution's history. Such hypocrisy may have gone relatively unnoticed thirty years ago when the Bank was not yet widely considered an important actor in global politics. However, growth in its size and influence lately has drawn the powerful IO into the world spotlight. Increased attention to the Bank's activities exposes its hypocrisy in its most overt and subtle forms. This results in a politicization of the Bank that affects its organizational security by threatening its autonomy and authority."

On the ground, Colgan (2002) asserts that the World Bank and IMF have been hazardous to health in Africa; and explains that "In Kenya, for example, child mortality was reduced by almost 50% in the first two decades after independence in 1963. Across Sub-Saharan Africa, the first decades after independence saw significant increases in life expectancy, from an average of 44 years to more than 50 years.

In the 1980s and 1990s, however, African governments had to cede control over their economic decision-making in order to qualify for World Bank and IMF loans.

The conditions attached to these loans undid much of the progress achieved in public health. The policies dictated by the World Bank and IMF exacerbated poverty, providing fertile ground for the spread of HIV/AIDS and other infectious diseases.

Cutbacks in health budgets and privatization of health services eroded previous advances in health care and weakened the capacity of African governments to cope with the growing health crisis. Consequently, during the past two decades the life expectancy of Africans has dropped by 15 years."

These figures and realities from Kenya were also mirrored by similar facts and events in Zambia, Tanzania and many other African countries where poverty ran rampant; in the words of Colgan (2002) and Githua (2011:73).

Confirmed by several analysts including Githua (2011:24), Chowdhury and Sundaram (2019), Voutsa, Borovas and Fotopoulos (2014:89), Odutayo (2015:5), Igwe (2018:119-

120) and You (2002:22); Allegret and Dulbecco (2004:2) write that "In case there is conflict between policies, the 'conditionalities' imposed by the IMF prevail."

'The limited and expensive access to financial markets for countries in the Global South gives leverage to Bretton Woods Financial Institutions over them, especially in times of hardship. As a result, Bretton Woods Financial Institutions practically dictate development terms for developing countries. However, despite Bretton Woods Financial Institutions potential to play a central position for development, these organizations adopted policies not necessarily in developing countries' best interests.' (Cepeda, 2021)

And so, "Suddenly, it did not matter whether a country did not wish to follow this policy blend; it was obliged to follow it." (Voutsa and Borovas, 2015:44)

The World Bank and the IMF have been said to ignore ""the Social Question" - in other words, "the question of how access to education, jobs and income is distributed in a society."
...In essence, the World Bank and the IMF ignore the fact that "social reforms might provide the most solid base for future economic growth."" (Reisman, 1992:S392-S393)

Despite having been set up with a development mandate and despite the fact that the World Bank started off building schools (Akyuz, 2015:480); Cavanagh and Mander (2003:19) argue that the aim was in actuality not education, but rather indoctrination with the purpose of later easily sell loans in order to indebt those countries.

For Noor (2015:81), "structural adjustment was a euphemism to a set of free market policy reforms imposed on developing countries as a condition for loans."

Nyikal (2005:11) further adds that Structural Adjustment Programs, "SAPs led to the postponement or total abandonment of development programs such as new roads, schools and hospitals"; in contradiction with the development mandate and mission of the Bretton Woods institutions – in general; and the World Bank; in particular.

Lopes (2012:71) wrote of the SAPs' "disastrous impact on social policies and poverty levels in many countries".
 This ultimately resulted "in the decay in the fabric of society", as Kayira and Hope (1997:118) describe it.

Muhumed and Gas (2016:43) agree and illustrate by saying that: "between 1960 and 1980, GDP per capita of Sub Saharan Africa grew by 36 percent, and then fell by 15 percent between 1980 and 2000. Between 1994 and 2003, the number of people living under the poverty line ($1 a day) increased 75 percent (from 200 million to 350 million)."

Furthermore, "In 1980, the total external debt of all developing countries was $609 billion; in 2001, after 20 years of structural adjustment, it totalled $2.4 trillion.
 In 2001, sub-Saharan Africa paid $3.6 billion more in debt service than it received in new long-term loans and credits.
 Africa spends about four times more on debt-service payments than it does on **health care**." (Cavanagh and Mander, 2003:19) [Emphasis added]

Parkinson (2014:8) spoke of the World Bank "neglecting the human impact of its programs" and the IMF appearing under the influence of "a small number of powerful nations" and "undermining its credibility with other countries."

Explains El-Tom (1994:9, 16, 17); the Bretton Woods institutions' policies have certainly been the most damageable "on the development of human resources, an essential component for development. (…) these policies drastically reduce access to basic infrastructural essentials including education, training, health and food. (…)

The rapid growth of these institutions is seen by many developmentalists as a handicap.

It has led to arrogance, self delusion and the inability to listen to alternative views, features, which are incompatible with development. (…) The overgrowth of the mighty WB and IMF presents a formidable problem for world development, particularly for Third World development. (…) their growth has led to their monopolisation of the world development process, a feature which can only have negative ramifications on the entire world."

Development itself appears to have been a victim and a casualty of the Bretton Woods institutions (Githua, 2011:24).

The UN declared several **Development** Decades 1961-1970, 1971-1980, 1981-1990, 1991-2000 as well as the Millennium **Development** Goals (MDGs) 2000-2015 and the Sustainable **Development** Goals (SDGs) 2015-2030 (James, 1996:135; UN/DESA, 2017).

The 1980s or the Washington Consensus years were termed "by many development commentators as a lost development decade" (Ruckert, 2006:43; El-Tom, 1994:21).

2.2.1 The Crises

During what Thérien (2004:12) termed "the worst economic crisis of the second half of the twentieth century": the Asian 1997 Crisis; the IMF's actions further fragilised economies and undermined democracy while blaming "the governments for their choices, their insufficient internal institutions and corruption of local communities." (Voutsa and Borovas, 2015:46) (Thérien, 2004:12; Daste, 2015:39).

'Poor governance', "institutional failures" or "state institutional weakness to create conditions for the emergence of free-market economies" are what the World Bank attributed the failure of its SAPs in Africa to (Lancaster, 1993:9; Cepeda, 2021).

In actuality, "Cold War politics did not encourage the development of effective state institutions and good governance in Africa" (World Bank, 2005:271)

Stiglitz (2008b:310) also responded that the World Bank and the IMF should not be lecturing anyone on governance, given their own track record.

For Lahdenperä and Humayoun (2010:26): "The sovereignty of the countries is eradicated by the composition of adjustments imposed by the IMF and the World Bank.

The governments cannot take the decisions demanded by their population without risking even more hurtful retributions. Monetary creation is frozen as the accountability of the Central Banks shift from government and parliament to the IMF and the World Bank. Monetary policy is no longer available as a means for controlling unemployment, exchange rates or interest rates by extracting and contracting the money supply."

On the specific matter of sovereignty; Matthewman (2012:1) explains that "the World Bank and the IMF used conditionality-based lending as a tool to control the political arena in developing nations".

Imposed on Argentina, the conditionalities, "included a series of budget cuts which has resulted in considerable social costs. The health budget has suffered an estimated cut of 8%, public services for women suffered a 19% cut and the public sector has faced massive layoffs, while the cost of living has spun out of control. The result has been a worsened debt to GDP ratio, negative GDP growth, small and medium-sized enterprises closing by the thousands, increased unemployment and poverty". (Saldanha, Perera, Romero and Brunswijck, 2019).

"During the crisis and its aftermath, the International Monetary Fund (IMF) was heavily criticized for its lack of support to the government. Despite several attempts from Argentina, the IMF refused to offer the liquidities the country desperately needed." (Aggarwal, Ries and Salvador, 2018:9)

The 1990s saw more crises in Mexico, East Asia, Russia and Brazil (Cassidy, 2002; You, 2002:13).

In the 1997 Asian financial crisis; unlike, for instance, Indonesia, Thailand, Laos, Malaysia and the Philippines; You (2002:15) reckons that China and India were able "to register spectacular successes in development by diverging in important ways from the standard prescriptions" of "the Washington Consensus' doctrine of the "free market."" (Saldanha, Perera, Romero and Brunswijck, 2019) or (Igwe, 2018:119; You, 2002:33; Cepeda, 2021).

Looking back, South Korea was a model of development; hardly ever in need of economic advice; whereas Malaysia waned the crisis by ignoring the IMF's prescriptions.

In Asia, some people "concluded that the I.M.F. and the American government had set out deliberately to weaken a potential economic rival."

Gwin (1997:249) confirmed those accusations, at least in relation to the World Bank.

"Over the years the United States has used multiple sources of influence pervasively, episodically, and often inconsistently in pursuit of both long-term foreign policy goals and short-term political and economic interests. In so doing it has been driven by contradictory but simultaneously held attitudes toward the Bank.

On the one hand it has looked to the Bank to promote development and an open world economy.

On the other hand it has considered the Bank but one of its many instruments of foreign policy - a source of funds to be offered or denied to reward friends, punish enemies, or advance any number of other objectives defined by domestic constituency groups or immediate foreign policy aims." [Emphasis added]

To argue that these elements have changed the nature of the relationship between Asian countries and the Bretton Woods institutions would certainly equate to stating the obvious (Vreeland, 2019:206; Cepeda, 2021). Especially, when it is further documented that "the World Bank and the IMF used conditionality-based lending as a tool to control the political arena in developing nations" (Matthewman, 2012:1).

For one, Poland transition to market economy was made by rejecting "a key element of the Washington Consensus: rapid privatization. Instead of rushing to sell off state enterprises, the Poles concentrated on creating a **modern legal system** and a **social safety net**.

Only then did they allow private investors to take over banks and the like." (Cassidy, 2002) or (Wolff, 2013:101) [Emphasis added].

Alongside Poland, Stiglitz (2003:114, 122) notes Hungary and Slovenia; and adds that most successful examples of development such as China and Botswana were without IMF programs.

Another Nobel Prize in Economic Sciences laureate (for 2015) and also former World Bank economist, Angus Deaton argues that "many of the positive things that are happening in Africa (…) are totally **homegrown**".

Echoing Stiglitz, Deaton reckons that recent poverty reduction in China and economic progress in Botswana have nothing to do with aid but due to the fact that those countries "**had to work it out for themselves**". (Swanson, 2015) [Emphasis added]

Easterly (2006), cited in Masters and Chatzky (2019) sees the benefit of that approach: 'client nations would be better served by homegrown, piecemeal reforms'.

World Bank (2005:306) also largely confirms Swanson's assessment of Botswana's progress. Kennedy (2010:473) and Cepeda (2021) are of the same opinion as Angus Deaton and Easterly.

Referring to what Aggarwal, Ries and Salvador (2018) termed "The Argentine Great Depression (1998-2002)"; and the global financial crisis of 2007-2008, Saldanha, Perera, Romero and Brunswijck (2019) accuse:
    "the Bretton Woods Institutions have often proved ineffective and, at worst, counterproductive".

An observation also made by Reisman (1992: S388-S389), Glassman and Carmody (2001:87), Thérien (2004:12), Chornyy (2011:34), Lopes (2012:71), Odutayo (2015:5); Toussaint (2020b); Arcelli and Tria (2021). As well as El-Tom (1994:7) who professes that "Behind the impressive and colourful graphs and equations of the economic calculations presented by the World Bank and IMF is a simple, primitive guru economics, which does not stand up to common sense let alone scientific scrutiny."

Especially when "structural adjustment programs (SAPs) have reversed the development successes of the 1960s and 1970s, with . . . millions sliding into poverty every year", elaborates Easterly (2003:362); echoing Noor (2015:82) and Odutayo (2015:2) who respectively explain that "The harsh economic measures further deepened poverty, undermined food security and self-reliance and led to unsustainable resource exploitation, environmental destruction, and population dislocation and displacement."

And as such, post-SAPs poverty levels in Ghana exceeded those before the program was started. Hence, the title of Odutayo (2015)'s article: *"Ghana Crippled by Structural Adjustment Programmes."* Although Ghana's was deemed the most successful SAPs in Africa by the IMF and World Bank (Lancaster, 1993:9; El-Tom, 1994:11).

What El-Tom (1994:7) labelled "simple, primitive guru economics" could be the July 1997 IMF advice to the Thai government to float its currency: the Thai baht (Wolff (2013:115-116).

In the ensuing 1997 South East Asian financial crisis; Indonesia, South Korea, Thailand, Hong Kong, Laos, Malaysia, the Philippines, Brunei, mainland China, Singapore, Taiwan, Vietnam and Japan were all affected; some countries less severely than others.

Furthermore, the IMF's rescue plan "failed as the programs it instituted were contradictory in consequence and exacerbated the impact of the crisis in countless aspects" (Wolff, 2013:115-116). Toussaint (2020b) concluded the same thing.

For Cepeda (2021): "the adoption of austerity worsened an already difficult situation".

'From the evidence on programme effects, it seems that the effects of IMF programmes, and the extent of their influence on macroeconomic policy, are over-rated.' (ODI,

1993:4). Indeed, Bird (2001:830) reported the criticism levelled at the IMF for taking on 'a development role, [and eventually performing] this role badly by hurting economic growth and failing to alleviate poverty.'

That goes to say that the SAPs – from either the IMF or the World Bank - were not entirely successful. Wolff (2013:129) wrote of "twenty-five years of failed structural adjustment programs for poverty reduction and the inability to assist major countries out of poverty crisis". In addition, citing Seshamani (2005:2); Noor (2015:81) quotes the 1988 United Nations Economic Commission for Africa (UNECA) report in order to illustrate.

"Regrettably, over the past decade **the human condition of most Africans has deteriorated calamitously**. Real incomes of almost all households and families declined sharply. Malnutrition has risen massively, food production has fallen relative to population, the quality and quantity of health and education services have made tens of millions of human beings refugees and displaced persons. In many cases, the slow decline in infant mortality and of death from preventable, epidemic diseases has been reversed. Meanwhile, the unemployment and underemployment situation has worsened markedly." [Emphasis added]

As explained by Wesley (1989:32), ODI (1993:2); Bottelier (2007:68) and Thomson, Kentikelenis and Stubbs (2017); even the UNICEF voiced concerns in relation to the SAPs' adverse effects on children and mothers' health in developing countries.

The UNICEF advocated in this respect; for policies "with a human face" (Ruckert, 2006:44) and for the protection "social and economic sectors that were essential to the survival of the poor, through the introduction of social protection programs" (Lopes, 2012:71).

Among UN institutions and organisations, the IMF and World Bank were therefore far from achieving unanimity (Thérien, 2004:6). Daste (2015:25) even holds the UN responsible for the World Bank and IMF's failures in terms of development worldwide.

Dealing with COVID-19 Recession - the greatest "since the Great Depression" - in the wake of the global pandemic; the IMF and World Bank Group faced with "a Bretton Woods moment"; took a series of actions (Serrate, 2020) that were deemed insufficient (Romero, 2020) and inadequate (Arcelli and Tria, 2021).

"The heyday of the Bretton Woods system, from 1945 until 1971, was a period of general macroeconomic and financial stability." (Frieden, 2017:27)
"During the Golden Age, between 1950 and 1980, (…) the World Bank and the IMF did not have development agendas" (Cepeda, 2021).

After that golden age which was felt everywhere, but in Africa and parts of Asia (You, 2002:4); the Bretton Woods institutions may have known many successes in general (Ruger, 2005; Kwagyang, Ghide and Haruna 2015:52; Odutayo, 2015:2; Voutsa and Borovas, 2015:44; Ibrahim, 2017:3); and in the area of development, in particular.

For instance, the economic boom of countries as Taiwan, Hong-Kong, South Korea and Singapore is attributed to the World Bank's SAPs (Dumitrache, 2011:1; Masters and Chatzky, 2019); with technical assistance offered, when it comes to China (Bottelier, 2007).

"The World Bank estimates that it distributed over $7.6 billion of aid to developing countries through international NGOs in 1992 alone." (Ibrahim, 2017:3)

Furthermore, in 2007; the World Bank was "the world's largest external funder of health and one of the largest supporters in the fight against HIV/AIDS". (Bottelier, 2007:69)

"The World Bank has had several successful interventions, in the estimation of many observers. (...) Projects span the globe and vary from digitizing health systems in Belarus to reducing air pollution in Colombia to generating solar power in Pakistan", say Masters and Chatzky (2019).

However, these achievements seem to have been overshadowed by series of crises, failures and criticism (Reisman, 1992:S350; Gwin 1997:273; Kayira and Hope, 1997; Osabu-Kle, 2000:2; Brown, 2001:139; Oxfam International, 2001:4; Colgan, 2002; You, 2002:21-22; Cavanagh and Mander, 2003:20; Easterly, 2003:362; Allegret and Dulbecco 2004:1; Driscoll and Christiansen, 2004:5; Stiglitz, 2008:47; Wohlwend 2009:93; Stein, 2010:6, 16; Chornyy 2011:34; Githua, 2011:58; Wolff, 2013:72-73; Parkinson 2014:5; Kwagyang, Ghide and Haruna, 2015:53; Heldt, 2018:568; Abouharb and Duchesne, 2019:2; Chowdhury and Sundaram, 2019; Arcelli and Tria, 2021).

And so Stein (2010:2) asserts "That reforms in the governance and policy structures of the Fund and Bank have been wholly inadequate in view of the **miserable track record** of these institutions." [Emphasis added]

In a similar vein, "Dreher (2006) uses panel data from 98 countries from 1978-2000 to examine the impact of IMF programs on economic growth. He finds that **economic growth declines by about 1.7% per year within the first five years of a program**. (...) More recent empirical studies have illustrated **the negative impact of IMF conditionality on economic growth**." (Przeworski and Vreeland, 2000; Barro and Lee, 2002; and Vreeland 2003), (or Stein, 2010:5-6) [Emphasis added]

Of the interactions between the World Bank, IMF and the Eastern European countries, it appears virtually impossible to empirically assess the degree of success or failure of the intervention. "There are virtually no econometric estimations done calculating the actual influence of IMF, WB or WTO on the countries." (Chornyy, 2011:40)

These comments are reiterated by Abouharb and Duchesne (2019:1).

"Relatively little research examines the economic growth consequences of the Bank's approach to development."

Igwe (2018:119) wrote of "concerns about the type of development plan that these systems will lead to and apprehension as to the role of the Bretton Woods institutions in shaping development". In fact, "the least developed countries have been in a Great Depression for decades as a result of these policies. (…) [For instance,] Sub-Saharan Africa per capita income fell by more than 40% from 1980 to 2002 (…) The number of people living under $1.25, the international poverty benchmark, increased from 213 million in 1981 to 390 million people in 2005 and constituted more than half the population of the continent". (Stein, 2010:16).

The reality was that development had ceased to be the priority in the 1944 Bretton Woods mandate (Helleiner, 2015:53).

2.2.2 Reform and status quo

Probably, in response to all the criticism (well-founded or utterly unjustified) levelled at the Bretton Woods institutions; they introduced the Poverty Reduction Strategy Papers (PRSPs) in September 1999. (Oxfam International, 2001:4; Driscoll and Christiansen, 2004)

Ohiorhenuan (2011:17) finds the related rhetoric questionable. "The developmental success of Asian countries was not based on ''poverty eradication'' but on the positive messages of building wealth and aiming to attain the living standards of the West and Japan."

Oxfam saw "this new [PRSPs] approach as an opportunity to develop economic policies which are genuinely country-owned, and which have poverty reduction as their central aim." Apparently or allegedly in stark contrast with "past economic policies for poor countries (...) worked out in Washington or between a small group in a country's finance ministry and IMF and World Bank staff. In such discussions, Bank and Fund staff have a tremendous amount of leverage because of countries' dependence on Bank and Fund loans and the conditionality associated with such lending.
This process resulted in the adoption of one-size-fits-all economic policies, which were often poorly adapted to a country's specific needs, which lacked broad popular support, and which failed to make poverty reduction a priority." (Oxfam International, 2001:4)

Driscoll and Christiansen (2004:22) noted some positive points four years after the PRSPs were introduced such as 'enhancing country ownership, including citizens, poverty reduction processes; beginning to tackle the long-neglected need for institutional reforms; and enhancing donor behaviour in the aid relationship".

Earlier in 2001, Oxfam International (2001:1) observed that "The Poverty Reduction Strategy Paper framework has not yet delivered better pro-poor economic policies in poor countries."

Stewart and Wang (2003:1) found that "the content of PRSPs is very similar to previous adjustment packages" and "PRSPs do not significantly empower poor countries".

Noor (2015:88, 92) is of the same opinion and talks about "cosmetic changes".

Matthewman (2012:3) indeed reveals that "closer examination of the HIPC-Initiative reveals that the control which has allegedly been granted to developing countries is only an illusion. The IMF and the World Bank yet retain a significant capacity to control borrower states' political policies, particularly those that are found in a nation's PRSP".

Along similar lines, and in apparent agreement with Yakubovska (2013:69); Daste (2015:40-41) reflects that in advocating the PRSPs "the priority is not necessarily given to poverty reduction or development in themselves, but rather to the integration of developing countries into the global economy, thus risking to damage the legitimacy of the World Bank group and exacerbating critics that it serves as an instrument of hegemonic economic interests. Through the PRSP, the very contested framework of global capitalism is consolidated as development policy".

On that very same note, citing Fraser (2005:317); Matthewman (2012:3) wrote of PRSPs "a technology of 'social control', which seeks to shape domestic political space".

"Actions by the IMF and World Bank give credence to the growing belief that the institutions "systematically act in the interest of creditors and of rich elites. . . in preference to that of workers, peasants, and other poor people."" (Wolff, 2013:106-107)

The Bretton Woods System collapsed in 1971. However, it was survived by its institutions: the World Bank and the IMF (Dominguez, 1993:391; Jin, Liu and Li, 2018:2134, 2137). Those two institutions have been deemed rigid (Mouhamadou, 2019:8); "arrogant" and unaware of their weaknesses (Thérien, 2004:12). They have fallen short of their original mandate (Daste, 2015:28). Hence the new mandate from the G20 to the IMF and World Bank; in 2009 and 2010 (Stein, 2010:8).

Possibly as a result of what precedes and in the absence of self-assessment, self-criticism (Irish Times, 2002; Elliott, 2016; Romero et al., 2019); the World Bank and the IMF still have a lot to do in view of "persistent poverty of two billion people and the chronic development crisis in the poorest countries." (You, 2002:15, 40) (Dag Hammarskjöld Foundation, 1975:25; Glassman and Carmody, 2001; Cassidy, 2002; Thérien, 2004:2, 10; Wohlwend, 2009:93; Stein, 2010:5; Dumitrache, 2011:2-3; Brundtland, 2020; Degnarain, 2020).

There seems to be an acute need for reform (Brown, 2001:150; You, 2002:23-24; Williamson, 2004:14; Stein, 2010:11; Parkinson, 2014:9; Helleiner, 2015:46, 53; Kwagyang, Ghide and Haruna, 2015:54; Birdsall, 2019; Degnarain, 2020).

The Bretton Woods institutions' respective missions and raisons d'être, as recalled by NBB (2014):
- "The World Bank fosters long-term economic development and poverty reduction by granting its members technical and financial assistance, helping them to carry out sectoral reforms or to execute specific projects – building schools and health centres, providing water and electricity supplies, etc."
- "The IMF assessments of the countries' economic situations and policies provide the WB with information which it can use to examine potential development projects or reform plans."

appear to be a long way away, if not failed and betrayed.

"From the outset the United States considered the Bank an instrument of U.S. foreign policy and used its influence to try to ensure that Bank practices promoted development in ways that complemented U.S. long-term goals and short-term political and economic interests. Although the United States is not the only donor country to use its influence to pursue national interests, the wide scope, frequency, and intensity of its pressure distinguishes it from other donor countries. Its position on specific issues has not always prevailed, but where it has defined an issue as a matter of priority, it has usually had its way." (Gwin, 1997:243)

Monopolist or near-monopolist, intrusive; "undemocratic at conception" (El-Tom, 1994:6); lacking accountability, transparency and responsibility; with loan conditionalities that threaten national political and economic stability; dominated by what Saldanha, Perera, Romero and Brunswijck (2019) and Colgan (2002) respectively called "the global north" and the ""Group of 7" (U.S., Britain, Canada, France, Germany, Italy and Japan)"; with the IMF infeodated to the US Treasury, its largest contributor (Gwin, 1997:195; Wolff, 2013:94; Akyuz, 2015:476; Igwe, 2018:121; Masters and Chatzky, 2019; Vreeland, 2019:207; Cassidy, 2002; Irish Times, 2002; Cepeda, 2021); the Bretton Woods institutions "had the flexibility to evolve with economic circumstances and take on new roles in the maintenance of international cooperation" (Dominguez, 1993:391).

They appear in need of new path and strategies for a more developed, stable and prosperous world.

2.3 Humanitarian organisations

ARTICLE 1
1. The right to development is an inalienable human right by virtue of which every human person and all peoples are entitled to participate in, contribute to, and enjoy economic, social, cultural and political development, in which all human rights and fundamental freedoms can be fully realized.

- United Nations Declaration on The Right to Development

Humanitarian action is probably as old as humankind itself. Its modern form stems from Western Europe (Davey, Borton and Foley, 2013:1, 5). Indeed, Henry Dunant's encounter with the harsh realities of war (Dunan,

1986:5) prompted him to personally take action, create the Red Cross and campaign for the 1864 Geneva Convention.

"Humanitarian aid" could evoke natural and/or (unfortunately) man-made disasters, wars, conflicts and then the subsequent relief effort. Emergency, life and death situation could be associated with "Humanitarian aid".

This study sets off to examine humanitarian organisations and action in relation to development. Unlike, 'humanitarian relief'; development appears to reside in the realms of systematic, long-term, methodic, calm, meticulous planning and then execution.

There is no development (planning, let alone execution possible and viable) during or in the immediate aftermath of a disaster.

In fact; after a war, a natural disaster; when the survivors' lives are progressively returning to more and more normalcy; what can be done to assist and support them on their new journey? In the next five, ten, twenty years and the rest of their lives?

Humanitarian actors active in the 'Life after the disaster' of the populations they are working to support are various and they fortunately appear to adhere to the same rules, regulations, laws, principles and standards the relief effort operatives abide by.

2.3.1 Development as connectivity and more

Development, as analysed here, is not GDP, GNP and so on; at least not yet. It is rather basic, simple, grassroots actions and initiatives that aim to eventually impact positively on the GDP, GNP and any other national measures of growth and development; by essentially and initially adding value to the lives of people (in time of peace) and survivors of natural or man-made conflicts and/or disasters; as their conditions improve.

As Hilhorst (2007) would have it, the task consists, in the first instance, of 'saving lives' and then subsequently 'saving societies' or even 'saving lives and societies'.

This latter perspective could equate to "development as a transformation of society" (Stiglitz, 2003:125) and development as "good change" (Chambers, 2012); especially through "building the state and institutions" (OECD, 2017:2).

Because, as Swanson (2015) reports it; development; among other things, reposes on "the strength of a country's institutions – political and social systems that are developed through the interplay of a government and its people".

That being said, Dagne (2014:47-48) reckons that "development aid has positively contributed to countries growth because most of aid recipient countries used aid as a source of income to support their development plan."

Nationally or internationally measured development does not just happen. Far from being a monolithic entity or process, development thinking has evolved. From the 1990s, it became apparent that "there is no one right way to achieve development" (World Bank, 2005:262).

Currently, development means and aims at "growth, human development, environmental protection, institutional transformation, gender equity, and human rights protection". (Ohiorhenuan, 2011:10)

To that list Ranis (2004b:14) contributes: infant mortality, life expectancy and literacy.

Ultimately, it is the product and, quite literally, the brainchild and the fruit of the work of all the people in villages and cities across the country. Human development "has a positive effect on economic growth (…) for both developed and developing countries. (…) human development is an important determinant of economic growth for any economy."

(Rahman, Raja and Conor, 2020:31). Because warns Alonso (2015): "Economic growth can coexist with high levels of poverty and unemployment."

Neamtu and Ciobanu (2014:32) see "correlations between human development and economic growth". Ranis (2004a:8, 9-10) also wrote of "a virtuous cycle of high growth and large gains in human development" as well as 'human development being a necessary prerequisite and a precondition for long-term sustainable economic growth'.

Together with Stewart; he develops further before introducing the concept of "vicious cycle".

'Clearly, there exist strong connections between economic growth and human development. On the one hand, economic growth provides the resources to permit sustained improvements in human development.

On the other, human development improvements raise the capacities of economic agents who make the critical contributions to economic growth.' (Ranis and Stewart, 2005:2)

'In the virtuous cycle case, good human development enhances economic growth, which, in turn, promotes human development, and so on.

In the vicious cycle case, poor performance on human development tends to lead to poor economic growth performance, which in turn depresses human development achievements, and so on. (…) Economic growth, which is an important input into human development improvement, is itself not sustainable without improvement in human development. (Ranis and Stewart, 2005:9, 13)

In other words, people make development happen; not countries and/or government alone: "development consists of more than improvements in the well-being of citizens, even broadly defined: it also conveys something about the capacity of economic, political and social systems to provide the circumstances for that well-being on a sustainable, long-term basis. [It is] a system-wide manifestation of the way that people, firms, technologies and institutions interact with each other within the economic, social and political system." (Barder, 2012).

This depicts hallmarks of a multisector, multifaceted and on going enterprise.

Development; at least in terms of humanitarian organisations, does for people – both after disasters and conflicts or in time of peace - what those people (will later potentially go on to) do for themselves and for their countries. Development starts with people or human development. Appleton and Teal (2002:24) note "the many and complex interlinkages between human capital and economic development". Citing Hassan et al. (2019); Gruzina, Firsova, and Strielkowski (2021:1) reckon that 'economic development is the result of the development of human capital'.

In the words of Chiappero-Martinetti et al. (2015:224), 'economic growth and human development are intrinsically interconnected.'

As such, development in humanitarian circles essentially takes on a human, humane and… humanitarian focus and perspective. Development "is understood as a process that enables chronically marginalized individuals, households and communities to achieve greater self-reliance in meeting human need.

Self-reliance does not necessarily imply self-sufficiency, but enhanced capability through economic, social, and/or political change. This is achieved through the expansion of physical, human, and social capital, expanding economic productivity, social organization, and political power." (Buckland, 1998).

While "humanitarian response is focused on the population (…), development processes seek to support the government and national development programmes". (AECID and DARA, Unknown)

Kopinak (2013) distinguishes
- Emergency/Relief (E/R) from
- Rehabilitation/Development (R/D)

"E/R is fast-paced, reactive, short-term, focused on meeting immediate basic needs and preventing morbidity and mortality. (…) Planning and actions are designed to produce rapid results through immediate treatment and life-saving activities provided by medical care, potable water, shelter, food, clothing and security.
(…) R/D is multi-dimensional and proactive with broad, complex parameters that focus on the rehabilitation and development of a vulnerable population through addressing bio-psycho-socio-economic factors within the cultural milieu.

Building capacity is a key component of development and can be defined as the transfer of knowledge and resources through mentoring, workshops, trainings, infrastructure development, etc. Sustainability is the ultimate goal of all development aid. (…) activities are targeted toward enabling positive outcomes for the target population through the provision of basic necessities, advice and mentoring with regard to health, education, equity, governance, infrastructure improvement and security."

Buckland (1998) agrees: "Relief is generally perceived as the short-term provision of physical commodities to victims of an acute crisis."

That distinction suits Beamon and Balcik (2008:5). Buckland (1998) further argues that relief and development "processes are diametric opposites". Kent,

Armstrong and Obrecht (2013:13) wrote of a "dichotomy" between relief and development activities.

Several other analysts see both processes as:
- linked (Buchanan-Smith and Maxwell, 1994; Ryfman, 2007:30);
- hard to tell apart and dissociate (AECID and DARA, Unknown:7);
- key to promoting good governance, the rule of law, respect for human rights, capacity-building; institution-building" (Studer and Fox, 2005:375); and as such
- should collaborate (OECD, 2017:2; Balendran, 2019); in order "to complement each other's comparative advantages" (WEF, 2009:20). To "establish cooperative relationships and systems between the two aid communities [can allow] to respond to the changing needs of people". (JICA ORI, 2017)

The EU, for one, is a staunch advocate of humanitarian aid, development cooperation as well as peacebuilding (Mosel and Levine, 2014:9; Medinilla, Shiferaw and Veron, 2019:2).

"Humanitarian assistance is beneficial to disaster victims and can play an important role in the development of the country if it is properly coordinated and responds to real needs." (PAHO, 1999:5).

The notion that "humanitarian response is focused on the population, while development processes seek to support the government and national development programmes" is not describing a synoptic, integrated view of both sets of actions (AECID and DARA, Unknown). Neither group of actors nor their projects exist in a vacuum. Standards that guide the actions of humanitarian organisations might prove useful and beneficial to states and governments (Oxfam, 2019:37)

As mentioned earlier:
- **Emergency/Relief** (E/R) would equate to 'saving lives'; while
- **Rehabilitation/Development** (R/D) corresponds to 'saving societies'.

In other words,
- short-term life-saving interventions and
- long-term efforts to reduce chronic poverty or vulnerability
(Mosel and Levine, 2014:1).

"Unlike emergency aid, which may be provided at very short notice, most aid is planned out over a much longer timeframe, and is aimed at building long-term foundations for **development** rather than relieving short-term distress." (Keeley, 2012:48) [Emphasis added]

In a view which could reflect the EU's mentioned above; the then UN Secretary-General advocated closer ties, synergy and cooperation between humanitarian relief and development efforts. At the World Humanitarian Summit, Ban Ki-Moon (2016:32) said:

"Humanitarian actors need to move beyond repeatedly carrying out short-term interventions year after year towards contributing to the achievement of longer-term development results. Development actors will need to plan and act with greater urgency to tackle people's vulnerability, inequality and risk as they pursue the Sustainable Development Goals. Development responses also need to become more predictable, both in programmatic and financial terms, from day one of a crisis, to ensure that a country is put back on the pathway to achieving resilience and national development targets as soon as possible."

Skills, new mindsets, visions, abilities, knowledge acquired from humanitarian organisations could certainly come primarily under 'human development'.

"A higher level of education, better health, and more income – which can be translated into improved standard of living and more opportunities – improve the intellectual ability and work rate of the labor force." (Rahman, Raja and Conor, 2020:31)

Alongside schools, hospitals, clean water provision and so on; everything eventually adds value to and benefits people, villages, cities and countries.

Would this qualify as a "Trickle Up" (view of) development?

Ultimately, development is human; and so it must be. "For a country to be generally recognised as a developed one, it also needs to be able to provide its **citizens** with as fair as it is possible a distribution of basic resources and services, such **as healthcare and schooling**." Karpowicz (2008:1) [Emphasis added]

Development encompasses many entities and actors.

For instance, "'When development is primarily understood as economic growth, then most of the money will go on supporting the growth of markets, supporting the infrastructure that helps markets work better,' (…) 'When the emphasis shifts to development being understood as greater human wellbeing, then donors have been spending more money on supporting the strengthening of civil society, supporting the attainment of gender equality, putting more money into education and health and so on and so forth." (Phillips, 2013)

Humanitarian organisations' priorities and perspectives are clear to identify.

The General Principle 9 of the *Principles And Good Practice Of Humanitarian Donorship* aims to "Provide humanitarian assistance in ways that are supportive of recovery and long-term **development**, striving to ensure support, where appropriate, to the maintenance and return of sustainable livelihoods and transitions from humanitarian relief to recovery and **development activities**." (GHD, 2016) [Emphasis added]

In the words of the United Nations Development Programme (UNDP), conceptor of the Human Development Index (HDI), "The HDI was created to emphasize that people and their capabilities should be the ultimate criteria for assessing the development of a country, not economic growth alone.

(…) The Human Development Index (HDI) is a summary measure of average achievement in key dimensions of human development: a long and healthy life, being knowledgeable and have a decent standard of living." (UNDP, Unknown).

Actors in this area of humanitarian action stem from mostly three groups:
- nongovernmental organisations (NGOs); for instance, Oxfam and the International Federation of Red Cross and Red Crescent Societies (IFRCRCS)
- governmental agencies; like Irish Aid, Norwegian Agency for Development, Canadian International Development and so on; and
- United Nations (UN) bodies: United Nations Development Programme (UNDP), United Nations Refugee Agency (UNHCR), United Nations Children's Fund (UNICEF) and the World Food Programme (WFP). On a related note, Matthewman (2012:2) professes that "The World Bank and the IMF had enjoyed an uninterrupted reign as the patriarchs of international aid since the initiation of the Marshall Plan in 1947."

As already stated, humanitarian action abides by well-known, clear, widespread rules, regulations, laws, principles and standards.

The organisations set out not to do any more harm than the people they are assisting are already experiencing.

For instance, organisations live by four humanitarian principles: humanity, neutrality, impartiality and independence (UN OCHA, 2012).

In the face of a disaster, an emergency or in the aftermath; while striving to put their lives together through development projects and initiatives; people still have:
- the right to life with dignity,
- the right to receive humanitarian assistance; and
- the right to protection and security (Sphere Association, 2018).

Even Second Generation Principles (Coordination, Participation, Responsibility, Capacity and Local Customs, Mainstreaming and Link between Humanitarian action and development) are pertinent to this analysis about development.

Furthermore; several, if not all humanitarian projects are designed using the logical framework approach, which among other things; involves end-users and people being assisted in the actual project planning.

In the words of Minear and Weiss (1993:35); "research suggests that projects enlisting local populations and institutions are often more successful than those that do not."

Stiglitz (2008:53) agrees: "The development of a successful development strategy will have to involve those in the developing world in an important and meaningful way."

"The Logical Framework Approach (LFA) is a management tool primarily used in the design, and monitoring and evaluation, of international development projects.

The Logical Framework Approach was developed in 1969 for the United States Agency for International Development (USAID).

In the 1990s, humanitarian aid organizations often required that a logical framework be included in project proposals, however, in recent years the inclusion of a logical framework in proposals is often optional. (…) The LFA is a process, the results of which can be illustrated using a logical framework matrix or "Log Frame".

Since the logical framework approach begins with planning sessions involving stakeholders and partners, it should be about people's priorities. Furthermore, it allows information to be analysed and organized in a structured way and thus functions as an aid to thinking.

Preparation of a log frame with the participation of all stakeholders helps to build a project in which all involved can agree to share the same ideas on where the project is going and why the activities are necessary. (…) The use of the LRA is described by DFID as being "…….about applying clear, logical thought when seeking to tackle the complex and ever changing challenges of poverty and need…."" (Malin, 2013:18-19).

In addition and in view of this study revolving specifically around development; points made by Malin (2013) resonates greatly.

"The LFA was intended to be:
- An instrument for logical analysis and structured thinking in project planning.
- A framework, a series of questions which, if they are used in a uniform way, provide a structure for

the dialogue between different **stakeholders** in a project.
- A planning instrument, which encompasses the different elements in a process of change (**problems, objectives, stakeholders**, plan for implementation, etc.). The project plan may then be summarised in a LFA matrix, termed "the log frame".
- An instrument to create **participation/accountability/ownership.**
- **Common sense".** (Malin, 2013:21) [Emphasis added]

Along similar lines, the International Federation of Red Cross and Red Crescent Societies and the ICRC, for instance, respectively state in its Code of Conduct's Principles 5, 7, 9 and 10:
- We shall respect culture and custom.
- Ways shall be found to involve **programme beneficiaries** in the management of relief aid.
- We hold **ourselves accountable** to both those we seek to assist and those from whom we accept resources.
- In our information, publicity and advertising activities, we shall recognize disaster victims as **dignified human beings**, not hopeless objects.

(Wortel, 1993:791) [Emphasis added]

Development is a right (OHCHR, 2011). And "genuine development involves actors beyond the mere government sector." (Manenti and WHO, 1999:12)

Humanitarian projects are human endeavours, and as such prone to human error.

They are only as successful as the people involved in their design and implementation.

Although errors and controversies in humanitarian relief efforts are beyond the scope of this writing; there appears to be a real sense of duty to learn from errors and mistakes.

As such, "a better understanding of the past will help ensure a humanitarian system that is more self-aware, clearer about its identity and better prepared for engagement with the world in which it operates. (…) The idea of using history to shed light upon the present has already found support within the humanitarian community. (…) Or, as Peter Walker and Daniel Maxwell (2009:13) put it: 'understanding the history of humanitarian action helps understand why it is the way it is today, and helps identify how it can, and maybe should, change in the future'. It should be clear that this is not history as prediction, but as preparation." (Davey, Borton and Foley, 2013:1)

Some humanitarian organisations and government agencies that are involved in development operate in times of peace. Others strive to lead people out of conflicts and disasters into more stable, peaceful, productive and prosperous times and places; because "There is obvious common sense in linking up shorter- and longer-term ways of assisting vulnerable people" (Mosel and Levine, 2014:18). Hence the concept of LRRD or Linking Relief, Rehabilitation and Development.

LRRD is not recent (Christoplos, 2006:26; CISP, 2006:4; Tamminga, 2011:2; Medinilla, Shiferaw and Veron, 2019:v; Mosel and Levine, 2014:3; Rama, 2017).

It aims at "improving this integration and ensuring a smooth transition between emergency (quick actions to save lives), rehabilitation (reconstruction efforts to restore the pre-crisis state) and development (actions to improve living conditions of populations with a medium and long-term vision). (…) LRRD was adopted in 2003 as one of the 23 principles for Good Humanitarian Donorship (GHD)." (Rama, 2017)

This approach takes into consideration populations being assisted's lives beyond the traditional, standard 'emergency' and/or 'relief' phases.

Indeed, Mosel and Levine, (2014:13-16) wrote of the broad principles of a good LRRD programme:
- Flexibility,
- Risk taking and openness to learning,
- Thorough context and political analysis,
- Working with local institutions,
- Joint analysis/planning and learning at country level, and
- Realistic programming.

Implemented by German Agro Action (GAA) in Sierra Leone in the aftermath of the 1991 to 2002 civil war, LRRD succeeded in creating food security in the country (CISP, 2006:6-7).

2.3.2 Continuous Incremental Improvement

> It was not possible to assess the impact of this intervention because of the lack of adequate indicators, clear objectives, baseline data and monitoring (ALNAP, 2003c:107).
> Cited by Hofmann et al., (2004:5)

> "Imagine an organization whose mission is to alleviate human suffering. How can you measure such an abstract notion? How can an organization meaningfully assess its direct contribution to such a broadly stated mission? And by whose criteria should success be measured?"
> Sawhill and Williamson (2001) in Beamon and Balcik (2008:8)

"If you can't measure it, you can't improve it." Peter Ferdinand Drucker once said.

At state, government and even Bretton Woods institutions level; progress, growth and development are usually measured by GNP or GDP, as seen earlier.

However, Stiglitz (2020) argues that GDP is the wrong tool for measuring what matters.

Quoting Simon Kuznets, the man who came up with the GDP in the 1940s, Stiglitz (2020) asserts that "the GDP only measured market activity and should not be mistaken for a metric of **social** or even economic **well-being**." [Emphasis added]

In the same vein, Alonso (2015) asserts that "GDP is a measure of a country's economic activity, and therefore it should not be considered a measure of a country's **well-being**." [Emphasis added]

That apparent or explicit allusion to people and human wellness might suit humanitarian organisations, echo their views and relate to their guidelines, charters and principles.

In their chosen field however, those organisations appear lacking when it comes to assessment and measurement: in humanitarian action, in general; and the development section, in particular. Although the latter is deemed better off than the former in that respect (Hofmann, 2004:3).

Humanitarian evaluation is not only of critical importance as it allows to improve the effectiveness of humanitarian actions; it underpins the organisation's accountability, transparency (Renzaho, 2007:17; Beamon and Balcik, 2008:5; Watson, 2008:9); and is also "an integral part of effective management and the PCM cycle". (Prolog Consult, 2007:14, 21; Watson, 2008:3-4)

The organisation evaluates *its own processes and their execution*. It evaluates *its own goals and targets*. The intervention's results are quite literally another matter.

Elaborate Hofmann, Roberts, Shoham and Harvey (2004:1, 5), "Assessment of impact is, in fact, consistently poor. [As organisations focus on] 'process' or 'output' indicators – on what is provided, rather than on its impact in terms of the humanitarian outcome."

"Aid agencies have long found impact difficult to measure. (…) Within the humanitarian sector, there is concern that a focus on measurement could reduce operational effectiveness, and lead to the neglect of issues such as protection and dignity because they are difficult to measure. Focusing on what is measurable risks reducing humanitarian aid to a technical question of delivery, rather than a principled endeavour in which the process as well as the outcome is important.

[So,] Taken as a whole, the humanitarian system is poor at measuring or analysing impact. (…) Assessment tools such as the 'do no harm' approach can also in part be seen as an attempt to anticipate the possible negative impacts of interventions." (Hofmann, 2004:1, 4, 2; Watson, 2008:4)

The aim of each and every said intervention is indeed positive results, effects, impact and influence. Which is why "The monitoring of a development or humanitarian programme (…) should include a review of how the programme is adapting to changing realities and needs, and not only focus on its initial activities." (OECD, 2017:17)

The concept of 'impact' itself still remains an elusive and potentially subjective one in humanitarian circles (Hofmann, 2004:2; Hofmann et al., 2004:1; Roberts and Hofmann, 2004:2; Renzaho, 2007:3; Watson, 2008:5, 6) as in the words of Hofmann, Roberts, Shoham and Harvey (2004:1): "Attempts to measure impact can restrict their focus to the intended effects of interventions".

Relief interventions do neither easily nor ideally lend themselves to "analysis and research" (Hofmann, Roberts, Shoham and Harvey, 2004:1); especially when faced with "the intangibility of the services offered, immeasurability of the missions, unknowable outcomes, and the variety, interests, and standards of stakeholders." (Beamon and Balcik, 2008:8)

The overriding principle remains the humanitarian imperative.

Delivering "education, healthcare, the provision of basic resources such as food or water" pertains to development (Karpowicz, 2008:1, 3; Ibrahim, 2017:3). At least on the part of states; or incapacitated, or absent ones that humanitarian organisations are supplanting (Ibrahim, 2017:2).

That being said some tools are readily available (Watson, 2008:4-5, 23-26), in general; and in particular for the development sector with the Millennium Development Goals (MDGs) or the Sustainable Development Goals (SDGs), as guidelines (Ramalingam et al., 2014:2, 3, 29; JICA ORI, 2017).

For instance, in measuring the effectiveness of development cooperation at the local level in Ecuador, the project used criteria such: Ownership, Alignment, Harmonisation, Managing for results, Mutual accountability, Effectiveness of development cooperation at the local level and Gender equity (STCI and UNPD, 2013).

Quoting (Hallam, 1998); Hofmann, Roberts, Shoham and Harvey (2004) list the three main approaches to impact assessment:

- "the scientific approach, which generates quantitative measures of impact;
- the deductive/inductive approach, which is more anthropological and socio-economic in its methods and approach; and

- participatory approaches, which gather the views of programme beneficiaries.

Participatory approaches are widely recognised as a key component in understanding impact, but have rarely been used in the humanitarian sector." (Hofmann et al., 2004:2)

In the area of development that Hofmann (2004:3) deemed more suitable and likely to engage in impact assessment; along "effectiveness and efficiency" lines (Clarke, 2007:173); the facts and realities appear to be similar. Hofmann (2004:3) qualifies his previous statement alongside Roberts, Shoham and Harvey (2004:5): "Even in relatively stable, developmental environments, measuring impact is difficult."

A related term and measure: 'effectiveness' appear unspecified (Willetts, Cheney and Crawford, 2007:52).

Explains Ngirumpatse (2019), in agreement with Ramalingam, Mitchell, Borton and Smart (2014:2), as well as with Metzger and Guenther (2015:1496); 'there is no common understanding of what development effectiveness means or entails. (…) A conception of development effectiveness needs to be articulated in its distinction with aid and development co-operation effectiveness. A development effectiveness framework is still to be devised. A convening platform remains to be agreed upon by the diversity of development actors with differing views'.

As cited by Hofmann et al., (2004:7), 'impact' in the development sector is:
"The positive and negative, primary and secondary, long-term effects produced by a development intervention, directly or indirectly, intended or unintended
(OECD/DAC 2002:24)."

It is not only assessing the effect of humanitarian aid which is difficult, so is measuring the real impact of development aid on recipient countries (Dagne, 2014:47, 50).

Thus, both the aid and development sectors still have a long way to go in terms of impact, results, outcomes assessment (Hofmann et al., 2004:7, 15; Ramalingam et al., 2014:2; ODI, 2018).

On a 'joint' relief and development initiative like LRRD, Mosel and Levine (2014:16) state that "the project would be evaluated for being a good development project – i.e. one that is closely targeted at **preventing the most vulnerable people from falling into crises** – rather than for being good at 'LRRD'". [Emphasis added]

In this context, Ibrahim (2017:4-5) states that "NGOs have shown success in providing services in many developing nations from Africa, Asia to South America."

In other words, the humanitarian intervention is not the priority or an end in itself.

However, for the sake of continuous improvement; the urgency and emergency of interventions; the Paramount importance of saving lives and relieve suffering should not be to detriment of quality; and measuring the real, actual impact of humanitarian action.

For both relief and for development aid.

"The absence of systematic monitoring and surveillance in the humanitarian sector is a serious obstacle to assessing the impact of humanitarian aid." (Roberts and Hofmann, 2004:8)

In the meantime, humanitarian organisations are more preoccupied with making positive changes: fending off hunger, sickness, homelessness, and so on; in order to create life-saving and life-improving conditions and situations, which would not or could not have been possible without those humanitarian organisations.

2.4 Summary

Tackling the Great Depression appears like the Bretton Woods institutions' greatest sole success to date. The European countries, former beneficiaries of the Marshall Plan are some of the most prosperous and developed nowadays. From the 1970s energy crisis; 1980s Chilean crisis; 1990s Mexican, Asian, Russian, Ecuadorian, Argentinian crises, 2010s Greek government debt crisis to the 2020s COVID-19 Recession (to name but a few major examples); one could ask whether those challenges could have been anticipated, and then quite literally 'nipped in the bud'.

The World Bank set off to develop the world. Instead, with her sister organisation: the IMF; what Heldt (2018:576) called "the Western-dominated Bretton Woods institutions" imposed policies which created and exacerbated poverty, especially in the global South.

The World Bank and IMF's 'long records as development actors reveal how these institutions failed the Global South'. (Cepeda, 2021)

"In essence, the purpose of the World Bank and IMF in giving loans to poorer countries is to assist those countries in raising their economy while helping to end the perpetuating cycle of poverty. However, the World Bank has been known to impose "Micro-Management" type conditions, which ultimately prevents much needed aid from reaching those actually in need of help." (Wolff, 2013:106)

Lancaster (1993), El-Tom (1994:6), Gwin (1997:205), Osabu-Kle (2000), Daste (2015:37-38), Odutayo (2015), Muhumed and Gas (2016) and Cepeda (2021) deem their intentions and actions imperialistic, hegemonistic;
- similar to bullying (El-Tom, 1994:6);
- contrary to peace, stability (Cassidy, 2002; Conte, 2005; Lopes, 2012:72; Toussaint, 2020b) and
- contrary to human rights (Daste, 2015:31; Odutayo, 2015:3; Vreeland, 2019:212; Toussaint, 2020a).

"The World Bank and the IMF see development as being synonymous with national economic growth measured by indicators such as GDP."

Odutayo (2015:2), on the other hand, views "development [as] primarily concerned with reducing poverty and promoting economic growth for all citizens".

For Mkandawire and Soludo (1998:142); "Economic development is quintessentially a political process involving the distribution of not only economic resources but also power. It is a process that taxes the political system heavily. It involves sacrifices and commitments that can only be sustained through a sense of shared vision and common purpose. It calls for the mobilization of national capacities."

In addition, "Development requires a leadership that is able to look beyond personal and parochial interests, and short-term considerations to the long-term welfare of the nation." (Ohiorhenuan, 2011:18)

"The idea of development articulated by the World Bank, for instance, is very different from that promoted by Greenpeace activists" (SOAS, Unknown a; or Karpowicz, 2008:1); and certainly independent analysts, intellectuals and humanitarian organisations.

To Henry Dunant, co-founder of the Red Cross and the father of modern humanitarianism; development "is based on a combination of education, cultural factors, and economic and political factors." (HLA, 2019:7). That view is also shared by Stiglitz (1998) who explains that "Development enriches the lives of individuals by widening their horizons and reducing their sense of isolation. It reduces the afflictions brought on by disease and poverty, not only increasing lifespans, but improving the vitality of life. (…) Development entails the empowerment of individuals, so that they have more control over the forces that affect their lives, so that they can have a richer, healthier life. Education and health are at the center of efforts at individual development."

In *The East Asian Miracle*; in 1993, the World Bank credited "especially education" (among other things) for those countries' economic and social development (Willis, 2011:61).

Unlike in most of Africa and in Argentina, in Thailand in 1997, "public spending cuts affected all government sectors, except education and health" (Cepeda, 2021).

Reiterate Boozer et al. (2003:3, 24); human development (health, nutrition and education levels of the population) is an end product of economic growth, an input "as well and a key ingredient in the development process". Rahman, Raja and Conor (2020:2-3) are of the exact same opinion. "When the capacities of the population improve, the labor productivity rises and positively contributes to economic growth… human development and economic growth share a direct relationship."

'Education, concurs Ranis (2004a:6), has a strong effect on labour productivity.' In concert with Stewart, he adds that "Numerous studies indicate that increases in earnings are associated with additional years of education." (Ranis and Stewart, 2005:5)

Besides, "There are long term effects of educating one generation on the welfare of their future children. Africa's earlier investments in schooling mean that many more African parents are educated. This is lowering child mortality, reducing the number of births and helping to maintain school enrolments despite falling incomes. The long-term intergenerational effects of health and education are an important reason for promoting social sector investments despite tight current fiscal constraints." (Appleton and Teal, 2002:24)

However; education, hence development – for one - has been a major casualty of the Bretton Woods institutions' policies. "The average number of years of schooling of the adult population in the LDCs was three years in 2000, which was less than the level in other developing countries in 1960. The brain drain is also increasing in many LDCs.

In 2000, one in five of the stock of "high-skill workers" in the LDCs, defined as those with tertiary education (13 years of schooling or more), was working in an OECD country." (UNCTAD, 2006:14)

Dr. Supachai Panitchpakdi, the United Nations Conference On Trade And Development, UNCTAD Secretary-General from 1st September 2005 to 31st August 2013 once equated 'empowerment of individuals' with the empowerment of countries.

'In the end, the sustainability of economic and social progress in the Less Developed Countries, LDCs will ultimately depend on building up their productive base so that they can increasingly rely on domestic resource mobilisation and private rather than official sources of external finance, and can compete in international markets without special market access preferences.' (UNCTAD, 2006:11)

Former Senior Vice President and Chief Economist of the World Bank from 1997 to 2000, Nobel Prize in Economic Sciences in 2001; Stiglitz (1998:42) is particularly critical of his former employer, and hence the IMF. He "referred to the disillusionment with the Washington consensus, which provided a set of prescriptions that failed to foster this development transformation. That consensus was too narrow both in its objectives and its instruments."

He adds: "while development is possible, it is not inevitable. Countries most successful at it – those of East Asia – followed policies markedly different from the Washington Consensus." (Stiglitz, 2001). In South America, Wolff (2013:101, 101-104) backs Stiglitz's assertion with Brazil and Bolivia's examples: they "challenged the neoliberal model and moved to a more nationalistic approach".

In stark contrast to this, "The IMF's negative involvement in Argentina culminated in January 2002, when the government of Argentina defaulted on $141 billion in public sector debt; this embodied 'the largest sovereign default' of a state in history.

The catalyst behind Argentina's default and economic collapse has been "attributed to **the country's excessive adherence to International Monetary Fund advice**"." [Emphasis added]

Whereas humanitarian organisations live by the Humanitarian Principle; Prof. Stiglitz argues that governments and their 'extensions' such as the Bretton Woods institutions make decisions because of "ideology and politics" (Cassidy, 2002).

So much so that what he termed "the neo-liberal Washington pensée unique" (Stiglitz, 2001) never delivered development, at least not to the vast majority of poor countries (Stiglitz, 2008:41; Bustanul, 2017:119; Cepeda, 2021). Masters and Chatzky (2019) add that 'the so-called Washington Consensus of fiscal austerity, high interest rates, trade liberalization, privatization, and open capital markets have often been **counterproductive for target economies and devastating for their populations**'. [Emphasis added]

In relation to African countries; El-Tom (1994:1) wrote of "the recent African development debacle". Dembele (2005) termed those countries' encounter and interactions with the International Monetary Fund and World Bank "a "disastrous" record": "since the 1970s, these institutions have gradually become the chief architects of policies that are responsible for the worst inequalities and the explosion of poverty in the world, especially in Africa." El-Tom (1994:11, 21) echoes almost perfectly Dembele (2005) above.

Emphasises Wolff (2013:114): "The IMF and World Bank structural reforms have proven to be inefficient and detrimental to the people in Sub-Saharan Africa. After adhering to the IMF's and World Bank's policies and mandated structural adjustments, residents of Sub-Saharan African countries have not experienced any long-term improvement in their living conditions."

"During the 1980s, 34 African countries adopted the Bank's and IMF Structural Adjustement Programmes. The outcome was simply disastrous. African performance records show that for the period 1980-88, per capita income declined by 2.6 per cent annually, while total employment shrank by 16 per cent. (...) the performance of the WB/IMF in Africa over the last few decades has been nothing but a total failure."

Weaver (2008) wrote of *The Fog of Development* and "The Hypocrisy of the World Bank".
    Easterly (2006), cited by Masters and Chatzky (2019) issues a similar critique.
    'The plan to end world poverty shows all the pretensions of utopian social engineering. (...). The bank's

attempts to rapidly impose free markets on developing countries in the 1980s and 1990s, known as economic "shock therapy," produced a **"record of failure"** in Latin America, Africa, and former Soviet countries'. [Emphasis added]

In what could be described as malicious, sabotage and hitman-ship; Budhoo (1990:4-5) reveals – for instance - that while dealing with Trinidad and Tobago; the IMF used "statistical malpractices and unabashed misinformation so as to bring it to heel".

The IMF implemented a "policy package that could never serve, under any circumstances, the cause of financial balance and economic growth." (…) Self-defeating and unethical as it may seem, what we have done (…) in Trinidad and Tobago is being repeated in scores of countries around the world, particularly in Latin America and the Caribbean and Africa."

Budhoo (1990:27) also wrote about the IMF "perpetuating the same economic nonsense; with the same catastrophic consequences" for Third World nations.

In a similar vein, Noor (2015:79) wrote of "The tragic failure of development policies in the 1970s". Matthewman (2012:2) observed "the World Bank's lack of progress on achieving economic growth in the Third World".

Lancaster (1993:9) talked about the failure of World Bank's SAPs "to produce a definitive success on the African mainland"; making that region "the poorest in the world" (Handley et al., 2009:vi; El-Tom, 1994:5; Wolff, 2013:113; Masters and Chatzky, 2019); with the world's lowest human development (Appleton and Teal, 2002:1).

Gwin (1997:268-269) reveals pressures on one of the Bretton Woods institutions, in particular. "Overall, U.S. influence in the Bank in matters of administration, lending, and development policy appears to have had a mix of strongly favorable and seriously detrimental effects.

On the positive side, the United States has used its influence to broaden the Bank's base of donor support; it has encouraged expansion of development focus and scope of lending; and it has achieved improvements in procedures of accountability and transparency of Bank operations.

On the negative side, however, the constant U.S. pursuit of narrow objectives, driven more by short-term foreign policy aims or domestic political imperatives than by concern for the effectiveness of Bank operations, has taken an inordinate amount of the time of the Bank's high-level management and has undermined staff morale."

Vreeland (2019:212) cites Abouharb and Cingranelli (2007) who "show that the Bretton Woods institutions have failed to promote human rights and that their structural adjustment programs have hurt human development".

It appears self-evident that there is no economic growth without human development: 'human development is not only an end-product of the development process, but also a means to future economic growth' (Boozer et al., 2003:2, 8).

For Ranis (2004a:1); "human development will have an important effect on growth (…) economic growth will enhance human development".

Heckman (2016) even professes that "Human Development is Economic Development."

Certainly as a result of all that precedes, NGOs belong into and are active in the Development Arena (Ibrahim, 2017).

"World Bank and the British Overseas Development Administration (ODA) have not only described NGOs as a development alternatives but also a key to democratization process which is an integral component of a thriving civil society." (Ibrahim, 2017:3).

Close to local populations and working at grassroots level, "NGOs can provide services that are much more appropriate to local communities. (...) they are able to provide such services more efficiently and effectively through drawing on local people's knowledge, and also using local materials. (...) it is believed that NGOs are beneficial to non-material aspects of 'development', in particular processes of empowerment, participation and democratization. Because of the ways in which NGOs are embedded in local communities, it is argued that they have to be accountable to the local people." (Wills, 2011:108-109)

For Lindahl (1996:5), development reduces the risk of, and vulnerability to natural or man-made disasters. NGOs support governments or even step in the vacuum left by some of those authorities for various reasons (Wills, 2011:111).

Humanitarian organisations, usually after conflicts and natural disasters, strive to create conditions to normalcy and development. "Humanitarian aid requires quick response for life-saving objectives, but development aid takes time to accomplish mid-and long-term objectives. Humanitarian aid acts according to the humanitarian principles of impartiality, neutrality and independence, while development aid is provided through the recipient government. Their ways of operating are very different." (JICA ORI, 2017)

Having said that; development cannot be *Made in China*; let alone be delivered by either FedEx or DHL. It is thought of, planned and implemented by people for themselves; at least ideally.

Guided by their principles, humanitarian organisations strive to put human beings first and at the center of their projects, both after conflicts, disasters and also in time of peace.

This work on development which is being crafted at the crossroads between people in need of relief and stability, local/national governments, international (financial) institutions and humanitarian organisations aspires to an almost universal and atemporal description/design of development; in an interconnected, sustainability-aware and human rights-conscious global village.

That 'idea' dates back to the 1975 Dag Hammarskjöld Report on Development and International Cooperation, prepared for the Seventh Special Session of the United Nations General Assembly.

"Development of every man and woman – of the whole man and woman – and not just the growth of things, which are merely means.

Development geared to the satisfaction of needs beginning with the basic needs of the poor who constitute the world's majority; at the same time, development to ensure the humanization of man by the satisfaction of his needs for expression, creativity, conviviality, and for deciding his own destiny.

Development is a whole; it is an integral, value-loaded, cultural process; it encompasses the natural environment, social relations, education, production, consumption and well-being. The plurality of roads to development answers to the specificity of cultural or natural situations; no universal formula exists. Development is endogenous; it springs from the heart of each society, which relies first on its own strength and resources and defines in sovereignty the vision of its future, cooperating with societies sharing its problems and aspirations. At the same time, the international community as a whole has the responsibility of guaranteeing the conditions for the self-reliant development of each society, for making available to all the fruits of others' experiences and for helping those of its members who are in need." (Dag Hammarskjöld Foundation, 1975:7)

Ibrahim (2017:5) notes that 'there are few empirical studies of the effectiveness of NGOs and especially regarding their development work. There is need for research on the outcomes of development work managed by NGOs in developing countries.'

Therefore, to be able to accurately measure the actual impact and results of development humanitarian organisations remains a high-potential, high-impact measure of those same humanitarian organisations' own success still to be pursued and achieved.

3. METHODS

This study revolves around understanding which organisations do the most for development around the world; and which organisations or who should be doing the most in this same respect. Alongside the literature, a survey is being conducted to gather the views of the general public. The outcome of the survey is to be detailed in the Results section.

3.1 Survey

It will have four questions as detailed below. It will be posted online on SurveyMonkey. Faced with the COVID-19 pandemic and the convenience of accessing the survey from literally anywhere and everywhere in the world, that platform is practical and easy to use.

It does not require respondents logging into any website. Upon clicking the link, the survey is readily available for completion (Appendix A).

SurveyMonkey is free up to forty answers and has data analysis capabilities which can turn the data gathered as numbers and percentages into useful charts. Once, the survey questions are completed and uploaded, a link and QR code can be generated for potential and prospective participants. They will be sent the link individually or in groups using the researcher's available channels of communication: Skype, Twitter, YouTube, WeChat, WhatsApp, FutureLearn, WordPress, Facebook, Facebook Messenger, LinkedIn, and InterNations.

The survey is targeted at a global audience of adults from all walks of life, professions, religions, genders and backgrounds. The number of confirmed and effective responses is beyond the researcher/surveyor's control; so about a thousand invites or requests will be sent out in order to maximise the probability of receiving a significant and meaningful amount of complete answers. The survey aims for the quality of the responses; in order to empirically assess whether the Bretton Woods institutions, humanitarian organisations or any other entities are more suited for development around the world.

The survey targets are:
- a population size of 800 to 1000,
- a sample size of at least 200,
- and 95% to 99% confidence level
- for 5% to 7% margin of error (McGill University, 2021).

The survey will be conducted for a period of three to four months, in order to gather as many responses as possible.

Question 1 - What organisations do the most for development around the world?

There are two possible answers to this question:
- The World Bank and International Monetary Fund (IMF) or the Bretton Woods institutions; and
- The Humanitarian organisations.

The respondents are given the opportunity (in the form of an "Other (please specify)" text box) to enter the name(s) of any other organisation(s); should these two groups provided above not suit them or match their decision(s).

The phrase "do the most" is underlined in order to emphasise its relevance in the question. The respondent chooses either the Bretton Woods institutions or the humanitarian organisations.

Question 2 - Those organisations you selected in *Question 1* <u>do the most</u> for development around the world because they:

- are accountable to their members
- have high standards
- are accountable to the people they are supporting
- are caring
- have sufficient funding
- have necessary political support
- follow a strict Code of Ethics
- have necessary skills, expertise and experience
- are politically neutral

Question 2 gives the respondents the opportunity to justify their answer to Question 1.

As stated above, they have 9 options to choose from. The options aim at representing the qualities and assets of the organisations selected in Question 1; which make said organisations a credit to development worldwide. Those assets refer, for instance to caring, accountability, standards, code of ethics and so on.

An "Other (please specify)" text box is provided in order to gather additional information or different options from respondents.

Question 3 – Who, what organisations <u>SHOULD</u> be doing the most for development around the world?
- Citizens
- Governments (local, regional, national)
- World Bank and International Monetary Fund (IMF)
- Rich and developed countries
- Humanitarian organisations (like Oxfam, Red Cross, Action Against Hunger, Save the Children, Doctors Without Borders and so on)
- United Nations (UN)
- Think-tanks

- Philanthropists
- Universities

Development is probably and ultimately a multifaceted enterprise and undertaking.

It is certainly too important to be left to countries and national governments alone. "Development strategies aim at introducing structural changes in a given context.

Their objective is to strengthen livelihood security and to reduce vulnerability."

(CISP, 2006:4). Even the World Bank: a "multilateral development bank" (Ruger, 2005:61); an "international development agency [with] expertise for development" (Akyuz, 2015:476); and "the "world's premier economic multilateral" institution" (Ruger, 2005:60) cannot do it all by herself (Kapur, Lewis and Webb, 1997:2). With or without her sister organisation: the IMF's assistance.

In view of this reality; development actors are or can/ought to be several and diverse.

A keyword in this question is the modal verb "<u>SHOULD</u>". It appears with capital letters and is also underlined. Question 3 states "Whose *responsibility, job, duty* is 'development'?"

The 9 options given to respondents range from citizens, governments (local, regional, national) to philanthropists, think-tanks, universities and the UN.

An "Other (please specify)" text box is available to collect potential different answers which were not provided above, from respondents.

Question 4 - Have you studied or are you studying International Cooperation, Humanitarian Aid and Development?
Have you worked or are you working for an organisation

in the field of International Cooperation, Humanitarian Aid and Development?
- Yes
- No

What is your current profession? (i.e. Doctor, Teacher, Driver, Mechanic, Lawyer, Student, Farmer, Unemployed, Cleaner, Veterinarian...) _____

This question aims at gauging the respondents' level of affinity with development, humanitarian organisations and the Bretton Woods institutions.

The question helps to see whether the choices are based on experience, education, information or are just guessed and hence random.

3.2 Results

The survey eventually was conducted over three months. About 1000 requests for answers were effectively sent to prospective participants; 442 of whom responded positively; hence a 44.2% completion rate. The sample size target of at least 200 was exceeded and even doubled to 442. Each person spent in average 2 minutes 58 seconds filling out the survey.

At 95% or 99% Confidence Level, the Margin of Error is respectively 4% and 5%.

Not all the questions were answered by all the participants. Question 1 was answered 419 times and skipped 23 times. For Questions 2, 3 and 4; the same pairs are respectively as follows: 432 - 10; 440 - 2 and 439 - 3.

Each question had a text box to gather additional, relevant messages and information.

The four questions respectively gathered 63, 17, 22 and 362 comments; a total of 464.

Question 1 - What organisations <u>do the most</u> for development around the world?

Humanitarian organisations are the most selected answer to the question above.

Out of the 419 respondents, 309 (73.75%) believe organisations like Oxfam, Doctors Without Borders, the Red Cross and so on are doing; and probably have been doing the most for development around the world.

A total of 143 (34.13%) people selected the World Bank and IMF. This almost amounts to only a third of all the answers. A comment echoes some of the criticism levelled earlier in the literature at the World Bank and IMF: *"These Breton Woods institutions have been created since 1944, what is their record almost 70 years later?"*

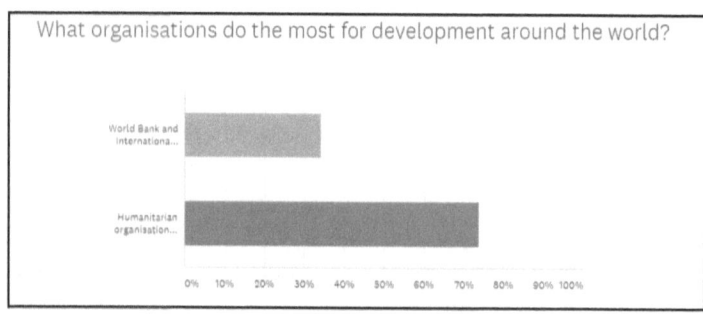

Figure 1: The Bretton Woods institutions compared to Humanitarian Organisations.

The text box below Question 1 allowed to gather respondents' comments.
Here are a few examples:
- IOM, UNDP, UNICEF
- The humanitarian organisations must be funded by the World Bank and IMF.
- Faith-based organisations. (for example Islamic Relief, Act alliance, Muslim aid... etc)

- Governments and Churches
- Non-governmental organizations (NGOs) which are closer to the beneficiaries on the ground.
- None of the above.
- UN agencies

Question 2 - Those organisations you selected in *Question 1* do the most for development around the world because (in order of importance), they:
- have necessary skills, expertise and experience (60.88%)
- are accountable to the people they are supporting (51.39%)
- are politically neutral (47.69%)
- follow a strict Code of Ethics (47.69%)
- are caring (44.91%)
- are accountable to their members (43.52%)
- have high standards (43.06%)
- have sufficient funding (37.50%), and
- have necessary political support (24.31%).

All these 9 reasons and explanations above seem relevant. They were selected by the 432 respondents, with close percentages.

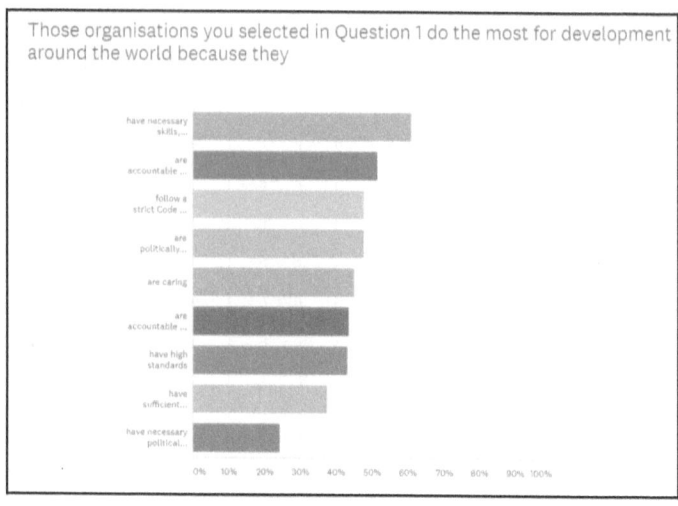

Figure 2: The reasons for selecting humanitarian organisations in Question 1.

This Question 2 gathered 17 comments. For instance:

- "albeit that none of them will meet all these standards all the time"
- "Giving Back to the Society Concept"
- "Are highly motivated to genuinely bring development to disadvantaged persons."
- "They act for development because they think about the well-being and the prosperity of humans"
- "They invest where there is potential. They serve the needs of the beneficiaries."
- "They come with less demands"
- "want to reduce poverty in the world, fight against famine, want all people in a society to live happily, to be empowerment and independent, want more justice, want all humain take they right as human being"
- "they have established as development orgs"
- "All of the above"

Question 3 – Who, what organisations <u>SHOULD</u> be doing the most for development around the world?

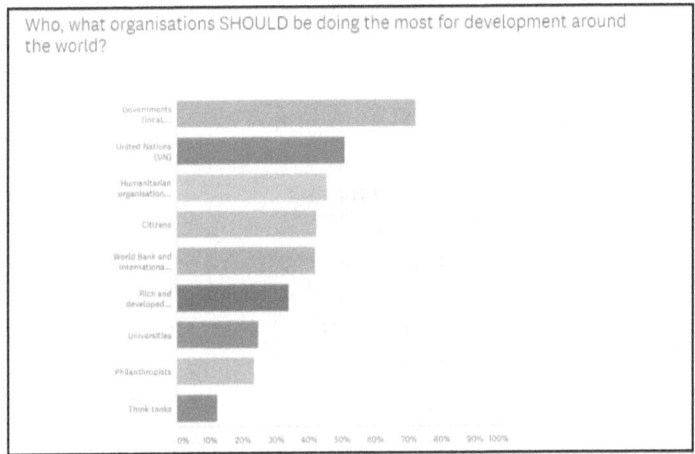

Figure 3: People and organisations that <u>SHOULD</u> be doing the most for development around the world.

Only 2 of the total 440 respondents skipped this question, making Question 2 the most answered one. In order of importance, it transpires that development seems respectively incumbent on:

- Governments (local, regional, national) (72.27%)
- United Nations (UN) (50.91%)
- Humanitarian organisations (like Oxfam, Red Cross, Action Against Hunger, Save the Children, Doctors Without Borders and so on) (45.45%)
- Citizens (42.27%)
- World Bank and International Monetary Fund (IMF) (41.82%)
- Rich and developed countries (33.86%)
- Philanthropists (24.77%)

- Universities (23.41%) and
- Think-tanks (12.27%).

Question 3 was complemented with 22 comments to "Who, what organisations <u>SHOULD</u> be doing the most for development around the world?"; with answers such as:

- "You and me"
- "All listed have a responsibility."
- we need a global response to poverty an inequality."
- "World Food Programme (WFP) World Health Organization (WHO United States Agency for International Development (USAID United Nations Children's Fund (UNICEF) World Wide Fund for Nature (WWF Doctors Without Borders Bill & Melinda Gates Foundation"
- "but without good Education in Schools, none of these organisations will have the support they need.'
- "Humanitarian aid cannot develop a country. In more than 50 years of development, which countries have been developed with humanitarian aid? The development must above all be endogenous."
- "Everyone"
- "People who love people and justice in the bible"
- "The UN spends more on itself than development. Working in the field , I have seen it first hand"
- "All have a responsibility in some respect"
- "The implementation partners especially the local ones."
- "All of the above"
- "Governments - Eliminate greed/graft"
- "Governments are accountable to their population in terms of justice, human right, equitable distribution of national resources and should therefore be doing the most, but rich countries have historic responsibilities on the current state of the low or lack of development in poor Countries."

- "Everyone should be involved in the growth and development of mankind and society."
- "Ordinary people, it is a worldwide responsibility, it does not lie with one party."

Question 4 - Have you studied or are you studying International Cooperation, Humanitarian Aid and Development?

The majority of the 439 respondents: 273 participants - and over half of them: 62.19% - have some knowledge, understanding of; or experience in the subject of the survey.

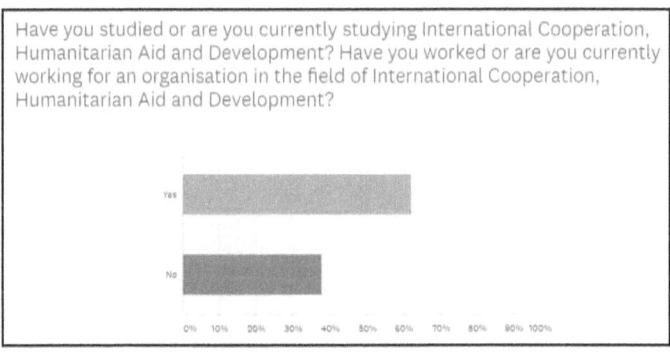

Figure 4: Familiarity with the subject of the survey.

Question 4 gathered the highest number of comments (362). Respondents disclosed their profession(s). And their knowledge and experience(s) shown here also helps explain answers to Questions 1 (mainly), 2 and 3. The respondents noted a wide range of jobs and professions. For example:

- Educational Consultant
- Planning Monitoring and Evaluation Manager
- Teacher

- Gender and Child Protection Specialist
- Publisher
- Doctor
- Unemployed
- Political Scientist
- Development Lobbyist
- Social Worker
- Retired
- Humanitarian Worker
- Psychologist
- Lawyer
- Student
- Engineer
- Humanitarian Aid/Development Worker; and so on.

4. DISCUSSIONS

4.1. Findings

Answers to Questions 1 and 2
Humanitarian organisations are the respondents' choice over the Bretton Woods institutions. NGOs, INGOs and UN agencies are most certainly examples of what the participants had in mind.

They make use of reasons, justifications and arguments made available in Question 2 to explain their selection in Question 1. For example, humanitarian organisations:
- have necessary skills, expertise and experience (60.88%), and
- are accountable to the people they are supporting (51.39%).

The knowledge of the people and organisations in the field is their power.
  Accountability seems to matter greatly.

Furthermore, in the comments to Question 2, one can read; humanitarian organisations:
- "Are highly motivated to genuinely bring development to disadvantaged persons."
- "They act for development because they think about the well-being and the prosperity of humans"
- "want to reduce poverty in the world, fight against famine, want all people in a society to live happily, to be empowerment and independent, want more justice, want [everyone to enjoy their rights as human beings]".

As mentioned previously, a Question 1 comment suggested *"The humanitarian organisations must be funded by the World Bank and IMF."* This approach might be aimed at combining the financial and political might of the Bretton Woods institutions with the grassroots expertise and ever-increasing fund-raising power - around US$ 25 billion in 2016 (WHS, 2016:v); US$ 3.2 trillion since 1960 (Fengler and Kharas, 2016:1) - of humanitarian organisations for the wellbeing of people in need. Indeed, three comments read:
- 'Local NGOs are the real heroes and heroines'
- "The Humanitarian organisations have more freedom to do their work around the world but they [don't have] enough funds."
- "I think UN organization with support from the World bank as a Donor for development work"

In the latter example, the respondent might be referring to the UN bodies such as FAO, WFP, UNDP, UNICEF, and IFAD; for example. Of the two UN bodies this writing is about; Igwe (2018:122) suggests a new direction and perspective. "The Bretton Woods institutions should be an embodiment of development for all participating nations with clear structured international economic relations guided by rules."

Willis (2011:108, 111) emphasises that "NGOs came to be seen as the panacea for 'development problems' by individuals from many different perspectives. (…) While many improvements can be made, NGOs alone cannot achieve everything that is expected of them." Indeed, NGOs have strong critics (Ibrahim, 2017:5).

Tellingly, a Question 3 comment says: "Humanitarian aid cannot develop a country.

In more than 50 years of development, which countries have been developed with humanitarian aid? The development must above all be endogenous".

A Question 1 comment echoes that local, grassroots view of development:

"I don't believe organizations do the most I think the most effective impacts are initiated by individuals at the community level worldwide."

As cited in Ibrahim (2017:3); "Mehra (1997) writes that, even though NGOs have been working in LDCs for several decades it is just in the past two decades that their activities have been directed towards development work and anti-poverty programs."

However, the know-how and experience of the humanitarian organisations seem to have been prompting a new partnership, as "significant amounts of multilateral and bilateral aid are now channelled through NGOs as part of what has been termed the 'New Policy Agenda' (NPA)". The World Bank, the UK government, the British Red Cross, Voluntary Service Overseas (VSO), Oxfam Australia and World Vision Australia are examples of actors of the NPA (Willis, 2011:109-110).

Answers to Question 3

Governments (72.27%), the UN (50.91%) and Humanitarian organisations (45.45%) are looked to to assist citizens (42.27%) make development possible and a reality.

Other actors such as Rich and developed countries (33.86%), Philanthropists (23.41%), Universities (24.77%) and Think-tanks (12.27%) are relevant and important.

In relation to the core of this study, World Bank and IMF (41.82%) are the fifth choice; even after Citizens. It is apparent that the Bretton Woods institutions have not been (major) agents of development, thus far; in many participants' opinion.

"Before the financial crisis of 1997, East Asia experienced three decades not only of unprecedented growth, but also of unprecedented reductions in poverty." (Stiglitz, 2001). The former Senior Vice President and Chief Economist of the World Bank, Nobel Prize in Economic Sciences in 2001 does not credit the Bretton Woods institutions for what the World Bank itself called 'The East Asian Miracle' (IBRD-World Bank, 1993).

In the light of the answers to Question 3, development effort must be inclusive.

It requires a wide range of skills, expertise (local, national, foreign) and political backing; in opposition to the Washington Consensus and in a nod to Stiglitz's "Third Way consensus":

- a balanced view of markets and government,
- a refusal to confuse means (like privatization and liberalization) with ends, and a broader conception of those ends – not higher GDP,
- not increased income for the few, but
- the creation of democratic, equitable, and sustained growth. (Stiglitz, 2001)

One of the Bretton Woods institutions praised some Asian economies in that respect.

"No one can look at the experience of Singapore or the Republic of Korea (and earlier Japan) without being convinced that purposive government action to promote rapid development can succeed." (World Bank, 2005:266)

The survey respondents, Stiglitz (2001), Quibria (2002) and Keynes, as cited by Willis (2011:39), all seem to agree on the need for government intervention in order to spur economic growth. This could be contingent on the fact that 'economic growth is a vehicle for human development. It makes no sense talking about economic growth without taking into account its contribution to human development' or simply development. (Alonso, 2015)

The UN Declaration on the Right to Development – Article 1 states:
"The right to development is an inalienable human right by virtue of which every human person and all peoples are entitled to participate in, contribute to, and enjoy economic, social, cultural and political development, in which all human rights and fundamental freedoms can be fully realized." (OHCHR, 1986) [Emphasis added]

As with other human rights: civil, political, economic, social and cultural rights (Browne and Millington, 2015:5); governments are the prime, the main and the first duty bearers in relation to the right to development and to actual development itself.

"Development is an inalienable human right" because development is the normal, basic and "By Default" right, state, condition, aspiration of each and every human being. Development can and does help fend off, shield or protect from vulnerability and precarity. In other words, "development is the best resilience-builder of all" (WHS, 2016:v).

Hinds (2015) and JICA ORI (2017) both agree on the importance of the role of the government. They respectively explain that "development aid is provided through the recipient government". "While humanitarian aid has generally aimed to save individual lives, often by working *around* governments, development aid supports structures and systems and is delivered primarily delivered *through* governments."

Ultimately, all these entities, agencies or organisations are there to support, aid or assist. Normally, there are no substitutes for governments: well functioning, effective, efficient governments. "In developmental states, government plays a central role in the coordination of development," rules Cepeda (2021).

Hence, the principle and the imperative necessity of governance (Appendix D).

"In its purest form it describes the structures and decision-making processes that allow a state, organization or group of people to conduct affairs. The most obvious among these is the government (…), as well as the administrations and groups that ensure its safety and efficiency." (Bruce-Lockhart, 2016)

"The concept of governance is not new. It is as old as human civilization." (LFS, 2021)

In an imperfect world and a country under construction, "'Good enough' governance is about effective states fulfilling certain basic functions, including **protecting people from harm** and providing an economic framework to **enable people to support themselves**." (DFID, 2005:20) [Emphasis added]

Sharing that same view, Amartya Sen, the Nobel Laureate in Economics in 1998 indicates that the essence of development is "the capacity of society to guarantee for its people the capability to lead worthy lives" (Ohiorhenuan, 2011:10). An organisation, Amartya Sen is quite familiar with – the UNDP (2001) – put the emphasis of development on people: "Development is thus about expanding the choices people have to lead lives that they value."

And so, far from exclusively being a matter of money or lack thereof, "development has more to do with the strength of a country's institutions – political and social systems that are developed through the interplay of a government and its people" (Swanson, 2015).

If anything; The Universal Declaration of Human Rights (for instance Articles 3, 17 and 26), The

Declaration on the Right to Development and the concept of governance, All aim at peace, freedom, dignity, fulfilling one's full potential as well as everything related and similar.

Answers to Question 4
The selection of humanitarian organisations over the World Bank and IMF appears like an informed decision. The majority of participants are familiar with NGOs, development, the IMF, the World Bank and the topic of this writing, as a whole.

There is a very strong; in actuality, a perfect positive correlation between respondents' answers to Question 1 and their profession(s), expertise and experience(s): topic of Question 4. The related correlation coefficient is **+1** (Appendix C).

4.2. Limitations

The number of people in the population was an approximation: between 800 and 1000.

The 'invites' or requests for response to the survey were sent on a vast range of media and platforms such as Skype, Twitter, YouTube, WeChat, WhatsApp, FutureLearn, WordPress, Facebook, Facebook Messenger, LinkedIn, and InterNations; at very different times, and in very different places; impeding a precise and accurate tally of all requests.

A very exact number of invites, even over an array of media would give a clear idea of the size, importance and significance of the sample. That would allow having a much more definitive, accurate margin of error; on the base of the *exact* population and, hence the significance of sample size.

The survey was intended to run for three or four months. It eventually took three months.

The length of time proved partially irrelevant; as the regularity and number of requests sent was the most determining factor. In other words, three or six months with no invites sent out would not produce any responses and hence impact the sample size and/or the number of responses and respondents. The online platform used for the questionnaire allows to purchase answers and as such; quite literally any numbers of responses could be available in days or weeks. The inconvenience of that approach is that all answers would be by US nationals; hence defeat the global audience/purpose; objective of the survey.

So, in the end; this survey run for three months; with an increased number of requests sent online to potential respondents; in all countries in that three-month timeframe.

Besides, the initial plan of three to four months would hold up the entire study and delay the analysis of the already gathered data or answers.

All the respondents were truly random: teachers, students, humanitarian operatives, entrepreneurs, retirees, doctors and so on.

The use of an experimental group and a control group could allow to understand the difference of responses from each group. A group of:
- humanitarian operatives (students and/or professionals), and
- all other professions or professionals

could possibly allow to observe if the background (studies, experiences and profession) has any impact on whether they see the Bretton Woods institutions or humanitarian organisations as more or less conducive to development.

A closely related and much more detailed analysis could consider
- age group, and possibly
- gender (male or female)

- nationality
- ethnicity
- faith and so on; depending on criteria the study is aiming to focus on and understand further; in relation to Bretton Woods institutions, humanitarian organisations and development.

Humanitarian organisations and development are truly human and universal matters. Under these circumstances, conducting a survey might require questionnaires in a few different languages; beside English, such as French, Arabic, Spanish, Urdu, German, Chinese and so on.

Interviews of humanitarian field workers and the people they have assisted or are still assisting could allow to gauge the impact of the humanitarian and development work; quite literally 'on the ground and in the field'; in support or in opposition to the literature.

To Question 1, respondents could be allowed to name some humanitarian organisations and possibly, subsequently the most active, productive, efficient in the area of development.

One could then learn more above Oxfam, UNICEF, the Red Cross, Action Against Hunger, Save the Children, Doctors Without Borders' projects and results on the ground, in the field.

This question allowed the selection of either the World Bank or the IMF. Even with the "Other (please specify)" text box; swapping the single-answer option for a multiple choice possibility might add more flexibility. A respondent could then select both the Bretton Woods institutions *and* the humanitarian organisations.

The draft survey had all the current Questions 1 to 3.

Question 4 was as follows:
- Have you studied or are you currently studying International Cooperation, Humanitarian Aid and Development? Have you worked or are you currently working for an organisation in the field of International Cooperation, Humanitarian Aid and Development?

Question 5 as:
- What is your current profession? (i.e. Doctor, Teacher, Driver, Mechanic, Lawyer, Student, Farmer, Unemployed, Cleaner, Veterinarian...)

These two questions were eventually combined, with Question 5 becoming a subsection of Question 4.

As mentioned earlier, the respondents' professions in the Comments section generated a detailed but extensive list: a total of 362 entries.

Options or checkboxes with groups of careers, such as Banking, Education, Tourism, Humanitarian Sector, Armed Forces and so on could be a viable alternative; for simpler data gathering and analysis. This could allow to produce a Professions' Graph.

5. CONCLUSIONS

The Bretton Woods institutions were created in the aftermath of World War II in order to bring about a more financially and economically stable and prosperous world. While the IMF was responsible for the stability of exchange rates, the World Bank was specifically tasked with development.

Akyuz (2015:475, 476) and Birdsall (2019) respectively call it "the largest global development institution [with] expertise for development" and "the world's largest development organization". The World Bank indeed prides itself on being the world largest *development* bank.

Overtime, the IMF took on some of her sister organisation's duties and roles (Bird, 2001:830; Yakubovska, 2013:72). Their joint To Do List spelled Washington Consensus, Free market economy, loans, conditionalities, Structural Adjustment Programs (SAPs), Poverty Reduction Strategy Papers (PRSPs), Heavily Indebted Poor Countries initiative (HIPCs) and so on.

Ranis (2004b:13) wrote of "disenchantment" with both SAPs and PRSPs.

In hindsight, the SAPs, for one, were probably not conducive to development; at least not in Africa. The SAPs worsened the debt burden and exacerbated budget related challenges due to the debt service. "While urging priority in repayment of debts, the IMF urges low-income countries to adopt potentially cataclysmic policies." (Wolff, 2013:134)

"The proportion of multilateral debt in Africa's external debt stock jumped from 17.8% in 1985 to around 22% in

1990. This increase, unquestionably, reflected lending associated with the implementation of the Structural Adjustment Programme (SAP) which is strongly supported by the World Bank, the IMF and other financiers. (...) between 1986 and 1990 the IMF extracted over $3 bn. by way of debt service collections from low-income countries in sub-Saharan Africa" (Ezenwe, 1993:37).

For Matthewman (2012:2), the World Bank and the IMF failed "to engender economic development in Africa, while at the same time saddling much of the continent with massive debt". Interestingly enough, in words that could evoke Budhoo (1990); Wolff (2013:96) wrote of "morally bankrupt lending practice".

In the specific case of the Washington Consensus, its conceptor John Williamson (2004:1) was clear. "The Washington Consensus as I originally formulated it was not written as a policy prescription for development". Even then, "Washington Consensus policies were applied for more than two decades in such diverse contexts as Africa, Latin America and Asia, as well as in countries emerging from real socialism in Eastern Europe and Central Asia." (Lopes, 2012:70)

It could be argued that the Bretton Woods institutions applied the wrong policies to development matters worldwide. Barely astounding, given the fact that "the Washington Consensus, was "not solely political in nature, but had its roots in the changing nature of the world economy"" (Wolff, 2013:120).

The World Bank's own views of development itself were limited in time and scope (Ranis, 2004b; Ruger, 2005; Yakubovska, 2013; Akyuz, 2015).
    Its choices and priorities were neither the countries' nor what they needed.

Heldt (2018:568) wrote of the World Bank's "lack of accountability and the inefficiency of its development programs".

Did:
- the former – "lack of accountability" - ineluctably and inexorably led to
- the latter – "inefficiency of its development programs"?

Only time and further research will probably tell.

Termed "the 'gatekeeper' for **development** assistance" by Wolff (2013:133); the IMF, for its part; targeted at ""firefighting" immediate macroeconomic problems" (Masters and Chatzky, 2019) was (initially) not set up for development. [Emphasis added]

Not to mention the World Bank itself.

Explains Gwin (1997:204-205): "as constituted the Bank was ill prepared to assume a major role in development financing. Its financial resources were too small, and many of the world's poorest countries could not afford its near-market rates.

Moreover, the Articles of Agreement prohibited lending directly to private enterprises.

As a result of these other constraints, Bank lending to developing countries increased only slowly. Pressure to resolve these problems led ultimately to the establishment of the Bank's two affiliates, the International Finance Corporation (IFC) in 1956 and the International Development Association (IDA) in 1960, but only after the United States dropped its opposition and agreed to support them. In both cases the U.S. endorsement was given **grudgingly**, as much in response to foreign policy considerations as to the challenges of development." [Emphasis added]

The US Treasury's influence on the Bretton Woods institutions (hence their global development agenda) has been made abundantly clear.

It could even be argued that the World Bank's original "bread-and-butter work [was] the financing of economic and social infrastructure projects"
(Kapur, Lewis and Webb, 1997:9).
NOT development, even if those projects (can) contribute to development.

One size-fits-all; almost inappropriate, unsuitable, not-built-to specifications strategies crafted almost exclusively at World Bank and IMF headquarters, with little to no national, recipient governments, authorities' input could be deemed both a failure and a recipe for even more failures.

Is it therefore really a surprise that the outcome turned out the way it did?
Today, is there a correlation between the countries subjected to those Bretton Woods institutions' policies and their levels of human and economic development; in other words: their HDI and GDP?
Do those policies have anything to do with "Africa's level of 'human development' [being] the lowest of any region in the world" (Appleton and Teal, 2002:1)?
Has the world grown more financially and economically stable and more prosperous as the result of the Bretton Woods institutions' mandates, policies and actions?

The survey conducted in this study appears to agree with the literature.

Henry Dunant laid the foundations of modern humanitarianism after witnessing the Battle of Solferino in

1859. Nowadays, humanitarian organisations are various and diverse.

They include Non-governmental organisations (NGOs), International NGOs, UN bodies and government agencies. They specialise in either aid or development.

Some are involved in both types of assistance; which this study made clear are different and require different approaches, timeframes and resources.

Relief efforts are usually shorter and more intense than development projects.

Primarily interested in saving lives, these organisations appear to be lacking when it comes to effectively assessing, documenting the real impact of their interventions.

They focus on changes which stop the situations they are facing from deteriorating.

For aid, and most specifically for development, which this study looks into; the lack of GDP, HDI type measures for humanitarian organisations does not seem to do these projects any justice.

Still, "it is better to trust the solutions which the non-governmental humanitarian agencies will endeavour to apply, because their approach has already demonstrated its capacity for innovation and continues to be developed in this early twenty-first century through action in the field, trial and error, research and experimentation." (Ryfman, 2007:45).

Henry Dunant started modern humanitarianism and Ryfman (2007:44) is predicting that it will certainly still be with us for many years to come. Especially, as "Humanitarian aid – whether in-kind or cash transfers – can have a significant economic impact." (Idris, 2016:1)

Visibility, accountability, responsibility, transparency, caring, an admissible degree of public awareness/scrutiny, admitting and fixing mistakes when they happen and then striving to learn from them and so on all matter. Humanitarian organisations are said to be 'innovative and cost effective, value driven organizations whose staffs are highly motivated and committed to serving the needs of the poor' (Ibrahim, 2017:2).

Consequently, the survey respondents seem to see and hear what Oxfam, the Red Cross, Doctors Without Borbers and similar organisations have been doing and are still doing; in line with the code of ethics, laws, imperatives and principles in force within the humanitarian aid or activity sector.

What imperatives do the World Bank and the IMF abide by?

Are they compatible with the primacy and pre-eminence of human life and human beings?

Are the Bretton Woods institutions any different from any high street banks or financial institutions? Ultimately, whom are their respective boards accountable to?

It has even been alleged that, despite their explicit and official mandate, the Bretton Woods institutions have been "development-unfriendly" from the very beginnings (Helleiner, 2015; Romero, Perera, Brunswijck and Saldanha, 2019; Cepeda, 2021).

Simultaneously, 'the 1997 South East Asian financial crisis demonstrated, many of the Bretton Woods policies were even counterproductive for development and considerably increased the social cost for vulnerable sectors of societies in affected countries' (Cepeda, 2021).

"The discord between loan conditionality and development objectives is rooted in the IMF and World Bank's governance structure permitting dominant shareholders to utilize conditionality as a means of furthering their own global economic and political agendas," says Wolff (2013:106).

For instance, at the height of the South East Asian financial crisis, it became apparent that the Bretton Woods institutions' 'objective was not to rescue the Thai population but impose a neoliberal agenda and guarantee foreign creditors' payment, including the World Bank and the IMF themselves'. (Cepeda, 2021) or (Romero, 2020; Toussaint, 2020b)

Masters and Chatzky (2019) and Cepeda (2021) respectively called the World Bank "the preeminent international institution for **economic development and poverty reduction**"; with "the board of governors, mostly made up of senior finance or **development** officials from member countries"; and a "**development** funder". Wolff (2013:133) termed the IMF "the 'gatekeeper' for **development** assistance". [Emphasis added]

It could therefore be argued that what has hallmarks of secrecy and obscurantism (alleged or substantiated); especially in relation to their development projects and activities and their "great intellectual arrogance" (Lopes, 2012:72) are ways for the Bretton Woods institutions – "the self-styled thought-leaders of international development" (Romero et al., 2019) - to occult their deficiencies, ambiguities, contradictions, duplicity, cognitive dissonance, incongruities, hypocrisy, incoherences, weaknesses, mixed and conflicting messages and methods, failures and inability to effectively keep their promise(s); let alone, pursue and achieve their own founding mandate, vision and mission.

6. RECOMMENDATIONS

Brainchild of Mary B. Anderson, there is a saying in humanitarian circles that states: "Do no harm." In the aftermath of the Rwandan Genocide, she wrote a book which title was inspired by the Hippocratic Oath and led to the *Do No Harm Project* (Anderson, 1999; Anderson, 2000).

Alongside all the other Charters and Principles, humanitarian actors strive to live and work by; "Do no harm" and even "First, Do no harm" (the original saying) could lay the ground rules for Bretton Woods institutions' operatives; especially in the face of the World Bank and the IMF's disregard for the human impact of their programmes and projects (Budhoo, 1990; Stiglitz, 2001; Parkinson, 2014:8). Humanitarian organisations' aim to saves lives and relieve human suffering in the aftermath of conflicts or natural disasters appear to echo the rationale that led to the creation of the HDI.

Explains Nayak (2008:1): "the expansion of output and wealth is only a means to development. The end of development is the welfare of human beings. Therefore, the central focus of development analysis and planning must be directed towards people's needs and oriented towards achievement of this ultimate end."

Poor people in poverty or extreme poverty; living in poor countries already face almost unsurmountable challenges.

"Do no harm" can guide decisions, policies and projects in several areas.

And so; if an initiative, a project or a policy is going to make:

- a child, her or his parents or carer go hungry,

- lack clean water; have no clothes or a roof; a hospital, a school: a future;

then that course of action should not be pursued.

Decisionmakers must find the (alternative), more humane and humanist path.

The one to a better present and future for each and everyone in the world.

Development by a for-profit organisation might seem like an oxymoron and an illusion.

Humanitarian organisations, for both aid and development have a duty to document, analyse and make available the data on the impact, effect, results, outcomes and so on, of each and every intervention. These figures can be beneficial to their own processes, credibility, transparency, appeal and their image in the general population.

Not just for donors.

If Henry Dunant could think of, create and inspire rules for war (the Geneva Conventions), surely world experts in universities and think-tanks; and under the aegis of the United Nations could think of Conventions for Development, mostly with regard to the World Bank and the IMF; and even states or countries. A partnership, collaboration and teamwork between those two institutions and the humanitarian organisations on development is most conceivable, advisable and likely (Balendran, 2019; Lie, 2020; AECID and DARA, Unknown:7).

Hopefully, the Monterrey Consensus of the International Conference on Financing for **Development** will be another step in that direction (Wolff, 2013:120; United Nations, 2003).

Precarity, poverty and underdevelopment are not only unsustainable.

They are as destructive as wars. In actuality, they (could) lead to wars.

Poverty leads to wars, which in turn lead to even more poverty.

Over a decade ago, IPI (2009:1) observed that "Chronic underdevelopment condemns more than 1 billion people to lives of poverty, illness, and poor political and economic prospects".

Whether that situation has improved or worsened today does not only remain to be empirically proven; but is also a function of who and what organisation is asked.

However, in the face of the global COVID-19 pandemic and the subsequent recession, the prospects might not to be great and promising (World Bank, 2020).

COVID-19 did cause a recession.

Bearing that in mind; and as already mentioned, with already poor countries more prone to strife and war (Stewart, 2002:342; Justino, 2008:6; Rohwerder, 2014; Swanson, 2015; Marks, 2016:1); the scourge of conflict appears ever-present; with potentially more devastating consequences.

Hence the urgent need of progress; because "development is the best resilience-builder of all" (WHS, 2016:v); and "the most direct route to achieving improvements in social and human indicators" (Rodrik and Velasco, 2008:324).

The empathy, caring and related emotions felt by Henry Dunant on a battlefield in Solferino in 1859; the vision, faith and courage displayed by the founders of the World Bank, IMF and the Marshall Plan; as well as the conceptors of the MDGs, Agenda 2030 and the SDGs all answer the call of doing a great deal of good for others and, ultimately, for all of us. That spirit is timeless, unstoppable, resilient and is likely to endure and multiply as long as there are lives to save and suffering to relieve. A partnership between the UN, (its bodies such as the Bretton Woods institutions), governments, citizens and humanitarian organisations is not only envisageable; it is necessary.

A harmonious, efficient, sincere conjunction and combination of best practices, funds, laws, principles, experiences for each and every human being could augur well for humanitarian relief, development and more prosperity everywhere on earth.

REFERENCES

<u>Books, Journals and Conferences</u>

Abouharb, M. R and Duchesne, Erick (2019), Economic Development and the World Bank. Social Sciences 8, no. 5: 156.

Aggarwal, Laira; Ries, Francois; and Salvador, Alejandro (2018) "The Argentine Great Depression,"Undergraduate Economic Review: Vol. 15: Iss. 1, Article 24.

Akyuz, Emrah (2015), The World Bank and the Evolution of Development Thinking. Akademik Sosyal Araştırmalar Dergisi, Yıl: 3, Sayı: 21, Aralık 2015. Pages 475 – 484.

Appleton, Simon and Teal, Francis (2002), Human Capital and Economic Development, Working Paper Series, Working Paper 39. African Development Bank.

Arifin, Bustanul (2017), The Failure of the Washington Consensus, the Need for a New Reform and the Rise of the Beijing Consensus. AEGIS | Vol. I No. 2, March 2017. Pages 118 – 130.

Beamon, Benita M. and Balcik, Burcu (2008), Performance measurement in humanitarian relief chains. International Journal of Public Sector Management Vol. 21 No. 1, 2008. Emerald Group Publishing Limited 0951-3558. Pages 4 - 25.
DOI <u>10.1108/09513550810846087</u>.

Bird, Graham (2001), A suitable case for treatment? Understanding the ongoing debate about the IMF. Third World Quarterly, Vol. 22, No 5. Pages 823 – 848.

Boozer, Michael; Ranis, Gustav; Stewart, Frances; Suri, Tavneet (2003), Paths to Success: The Relationship Between Human Development and Economic Growth.
Center Discussion Paper, No. 874, Yale University, Economic Growth Center, New Haven, CT.

Bottelier, Pieter (2007), China and the World Bank: how a partnership was built. Journal of Contemporary China, 16:51. Pages 239 - 258,
DOI: 10.1080/10670560701194475

Brown, Bartram S. (2001), IMF Governance, the Asian Financial Crisis, and the New International Financial Architecture.
In: International law in the post-cold war world: essays in memory of Li Haopei.
London; New York: Routledge, 2001. Pages 131-147.

Browne, E and Millington, K. A. (2015). Social development and human development: Topic guide. Birmingham / Oxford: GSDRC, University of Birmingham / HEART.

Buchanan-Smith, Margaret and Maxwell, Simon (1994), Linking Relief and Development: An Introduction and Overview. IDS Bulletin Volume 25, Issue 4; October 1994. IDS Bulletin. Pages 2 - 16.

Budhoo, Davison L. (1990), Enough Is Enough: Dear Mr. Camdessus. . . Open Letter of Resignation to the Managing Director of the International Monetary Fund (New York: New Horizons Press, 1990), 102.
Cavanagh, John and Mander, Jerry (2003), World Bank, IMF turned poor Third World nations into loan addicts. A Critique Of Corporate Globalization (Part III).
The CCPA Monitor. July/August 2003. Pages 19 – 22.

Cavanagh, John and Mander, Jerry (2003), World Bank, IMF turned poor Third World nations into loan addicts. A Critique Of Corporate Globalization (Part III). The CCPA Monitor. July/August 2003. Pages 19 – 22.

Chiappero-Martinetti E., von Jacobi N., Signorelli M. (2015), Human Development and Economic Growth. In: Hölscher J., Tomann H. (eds) Palgrave Dictionary of Emerging Markets and Transition Economics. Palgrave Macmillan, London.
DOI: https://doi.org/10.1007/978-1-137-37138-6_13

Christoplos, C. (2006), Links between relief, rehabilitation and development in the tsunami response. London: Tsunami Evaluation Coalition. ISBN: 0 85003 810 3.

Chornyy, Oleksandr (2011), Influence of the Bretton Woods Institutions on Economic Growth: Literature Survey for Transitional Economic Systems. Economics and Sociology, Vol. 4, No 2, 2011, pp. 32-41. ISSN 2071-789X

CISP (International Committee for the Development of Peoples), (2006), Linking relief to rehabilitation and development: what does it mean today?
In Voice Out Loud Issue 4 - Linking Relief To Rehabilitation And Development. December 2006.

Clarke, Matthew (2007), Raising The Funds – Spending The Funds: A Case Study Of The Effectiveness Of Both Roles Of NGOs. In "Measuring Effectiveness In Humanitarian And Development Aid: Conceptual Frameworks, Principles And Practice." Edited by Andre M. N. Renzaho. Nova Science Publishers, Inc. ISBN 978-1-60021-959-7. Pages 173 – 185.

Conte, B. (2005). La responsabilité du fmi et de la Banque mondiale dans le conflit en Côte d'Ivoire. Études internationales, 36(2), 219–229.
https://doi.org/10.7202/011416ar

Dag Hammarskjöld Foundation (1975), What Now: the 1975 Dag Hammarskjöld Report on Development and International Cooperation, prepared for the Seventh Special Session of the United Nations General Assembly - New York, 1-12 September 1975. Uppsala: Dag Hammarskjöld Foundation.

Davey, Eleanor; Borton, John and Foley, Matthew (2013), A history of the humanitarian system Western origins and foundations. HPG Working Paper June 2013. Humanitarian Policy Group Overseas Development Institute. London. ISBN: 978 1 909464 36 0.

Dembele, Demba Moussa (2005), The International Monetary Fund and World Bank in Africa: a "disastrous" record. In International Journal of Health Services. 2005; 35 (2). Pages 389 - 398. DOI: 10.2190/QVBH-WXP0-9NVP-8FW3. PMID: 15932012.

Dominguez, Kathryn M.E. (1993), The Role of International Organizations in the Bretton Woods System. In "A Retrospective on the Bretton Woods System: Lessons for International Monetary Reform" Edited by Michael D. Bordo and Barry Eichengreen. University of Chicago Press. ISBN 0-226-06587-1. Pages 357- 404.

Department for International Development, DFID (2005), Why we need to work more effectively in fragile states. London – Glasgow. ISBN: 1 86192 667 7.

Duffy, David (2002), Underdevelopment and Less Developed Countries. In Student Economic Review (SER). Trinity College Dublin, The University of Dublin. Pages 253 – 263.

Dunant, Henry (1986), A Memory from Solferino. International Committee of the Red Cross. ICRC publication 1986 ref. 0361 By Henry Dunant.

Easterly, William (2003), IMF and World Bank Structural Adjustment Programs and Poverty. In "Managing Currency Crises In Emerging Markets". Edited By Michael P. Dooley And Jeffrey A. Frankel. University Of Chicago Press. ISBN 0-226-15540-4.
Pages 361 – 391.

Ezenwe, Uka (1993), The African debt crisis and the challenge of development. Intereconomics, Nomos Verlagsgesellschaft, Baden-Baden, Vol. 28, Iss. 1. ISSN 0020-5346. Pages 35 – 43.
DOI: http://dx.doi.org/10.1007/BF02928100

Glassman, Jim and Carmody, Pádraig (2001), Structural adjustment in East and Southeast Asia: Lessons from Latin America. Geoforum. 32. 77-90.
DOI: 10.1016/S0016-7185(00)00039-7.

Gruzina, Yulia; Irina, Firsova and Wadim, Strielkowski (2021), Dynamics of Human Capital Development in Economic Development Cycles.
ECONOMIES 9, no. 2: 67.
DOI: https://doi.org/10.3390/economies9020067

Gwin, Catherine (1997), US Relations with the World Bank, 1945-1992.
Chapter Six In Kapur, D., Lewis, J. P. and Webb, R. (1997), The World Bank. Its First Half Century, Volume 2: Perspectives. Washington, DC: Brookings Institution. ISBN 0-8157-5236-9. Pages 195 – 274.

Handley, Geoff; Higgins, Kate; Sharma, Bhavna; Bird, Kate and Cammack, Diana (2009), Poverty and poverty reduction in sub-Saharan Africa: An overview of the issues. Working Paper 299 Results of ODI research presented in preliminary form for discussion and critical comment. January 2009. Overseas Development Institute (ODI). London. ISBN 978 0 85003 895 8.

Heldt, Eugénia C. (2018), Lost in internal evaluation? Accountability and insulation at the World Bank. Contemporary Politics, 24:5, 568-587
DOI: 10.1080/13569775.2018.1455491

Helleiner, Eric (2015), Restoring The Development Dimension Of Bretton Woods Rethinking Development Strategies after the Financial Crisis – Volume I: Making the Case for Policy Space. Edited by Edited by Alfredo Calcagno, Sebastian Dullien, Alejandro Márquez-Velázquez, Nicolas Maystre and Jan Priewe.
UNCTAD/GDS/MDP/2015/1. Pages 45 – 54.

Hicks, Norman and Streeten, Paul (1979), Indicators of Development: The Search for a Basic Needs Yardstick. World Development Vol. 7, pp. 567-580 Pergamon Press Ltd.

Hinds, R. (2015), Relationship between humanitarian and development aid (GSDRC Helpdesk Research Report 1185). Birmingham, UK: GSDRC, University of Birmingham.

Hofmann, Charles-Antoine (2004), Measuring the impact of humanitarian aid. A review of current practice. Researched, written and published by the Humanitarian Policy Group at the Overseas Development Institute (ODI). Number 15, June 2004. London.

Hofmann, Charles-Antoine; Roberts, Les; Shoham, Jeremy and Harvey, Paul (2004), Measuring the impact of humanitarian aid. A review of current practice.
Researched, written and published by the Humanitarian Policy Group at the Overseas Development Institute (ODI). Report 17, June 2004. London.

Idris, I. (2016), Economic impacts of humanitarian aid (GSDRC Helpdesk Research Report 1327). Birmingham, UK: GSDRC, University of Birmingham.

Igwe, Isaac O.C. (2018), History of the International Economy: The Bretton Woods System and its Impact on the Economic Development of Developing Countries.
Athens Journal of Law - Volume 4, Issue 2. Pages 105-126.

International Bank for Reconstruction and Development (IBRD)/World Bank (1993), The East Asian Miracle. Economic Growth and Public Policy.
Published for the World Bank Oxford University Press. ISBN 0-19-520993-1

International Peace Institute (IPI) (2009), Underdevelopment, Resource Scarcity, and Environmental Degradation. IPI Blue Paper No. 1, Task Forces on Strengthening Multilateral Security Capacity, New York, 2009.

James, Harold (1996), Development and Bretton Woods. In "From Bretton Woods to the Information Age." Oxford University Press.
ISBN: 9781475506969. Pages 586 - 620.
DOI: https://doi.org/10.5089/9781475506969.071

James, Harold (1996), Development and Bretton Woods. In "International Monetary Cooperation Since Bretton Woods." Oxford University Press.
ISBN: 9781475506969. Pages 120 - 147.
DOI: https://doi.org/10.5089/9781475506969.071

Justino, Patricia (2008), Poverty and Violent Conflict: A Micro-Level Perspective on the Causes and Duration of Warfare. Households in Conflict Network, HiCN Working Papers. 46.
DOI: 10.2139/ssrn.1142802.

Kapur, D., Lewis, J. P. and Webb, R. (1997), The World Bank. Its First Half Century,
Volume 2: Perspectives. Washington, DC: Brookings Institution. ISBN 0-8157-5236-9

Kayira, G and Hope, K.R. (1997), Development Policies in Southern Africa: The Impact of Structural Adjustment Programmes. South African Journal of Economics 65(2). Pages 118 - 126.
DOI: 10.1111/j.1813-6982.1997.tb01363.x

Keeley, Brian (2012), What is aid?
In From Aid to Development: The Global Fight against Poverty. OECD Publishing, Paris.
DOI: https://doi.org/10.1787/9789264123571-4-en

Kennedy, Scott (2010), The Myth of the Beijing Consensus, Journal of Contemporary China, 19:65. Pages 461 – 477. DOI: 10.1080/10670561003666087

Kent, Randolph; Armstrong, Justin and Obrecht, Alice (2013), The Future of Non-Governmental Organisations in the Humanitarian Sector. Humanitarian Futures Programme. Humanitarian Futures Programme, King's College London August 2013.

Lancaster, Carol (1993), Governance And Development: The Views From Washington.
IDS Bulletin, vol 24, no 1, 1993. Pages 9 – 15.

Lancaster, Carol (1997), The World Bank in Africa since 1980: The Politics of Structural Adjustment Lending. Chapter Five In Kapur, D., Lewis, J. P. and Webb, R. (1997), The World Bank. Its First Half Century, Volume 2: Perspectives. Washington, DC: Brookings Institution. ISBN 0-8157-5236-9. Pages 161 – 194.

Lie, J.H.S. (2020), The humanitarian-development nexus: humanitarian principles, practice, and pragmatics. Int J Humanitarian Action 5, 18 (2020).
https://doi.org/10.1186/s41018-020-00086-0

Lindahl, C. (1996), Developmental Relief?
An Issues Paper and an Annotated Bibliography on Linking Relief and Development.
SIDA. Stockholm. ISSN 1402-215X.

Lopes, Carlos (2012), Economic Growth and Inequality: The New Post-Washington Consensus. RCCS Annual Review, 4, October 2012: 69-85.

Manenti, Ambrogio and World Health Organization. Regional Office for Europe (1999), Decentralised co-operation: a new tool for conflict situations - the experience of WHO in Bosnia and Herzegovina: a case study by Ambrogio Manenti.
World Health Organization: Regional Office for Europe.

Marks, Z. (2016), Conflict and poverty. GSDRC Professional Development Reading
Pack no. 52. Birmingham, UK: University of Birmingham.

Medinilla, Alfonso; Shiferaw, Lidet Tadesse and Veron, Pauline (2019), Think local. Governance, humanitarian aid, development and peacebuilding in Somalia. European Centre for Development Policy Management, ECDPM. Making policies work Discussion Paper No. 246. March 2019. ISSN1571-7577.

Metzger, Laura and Guenther, Isabel (2015), How To Assess The Effectiveness Of Development Aid Projects: Evaluation Ratings Versus Project Indicators. Journal of International Development, 27, 1496–1520 (2015). Published online in Wiley Online Library. DOI: 10.1002/jid.3189

Minear, Larry and Weiss, Thomas (1993), Humanitarian Principles and Operational Dilemmas in War Zones - Trainer's Guide - 1st Edition (Disaster Management Training Programme). GE.94-02887.

Mkandawire, Thandika and Soludo, Charles C. (1998), Our Continent, Our Future. African Perspectives on Structural Adjustment. CODESRIA, Africa World Press, IDRC. ISBN 2-86978-074-5.

Moghalu, Kingsley Chiedu (2019), Bretton Woods, the West and the rest. In Bretton Woods: the next 70 years. Published by the Reinventing Bretton Woods Committee. Pages 239 – 246.

Mosel, Irina and Levine, Simon (2014), Remaking the case for linking relief, rehabilitation and development. How LRRD can become a practically useful concept for assistance in difficult places. HPG Commissioned Report. Humanitarian Policy Group, Overseas Development Institute. London. ISBN: 978 1 909464 67 4.

Mouhamadou, M. LY (2019), Bretton Woods's system: did we throw the baby out with the bathwater? Lessons for developing economies. Policy Center for the New South. Policy Brief. May 2019, PB-19/18.

Muhumed, Mohamed Muhumed and Gas, Sayid (2016), The World Bank and IMF in Developing Countries: Helping or Hindering? International Journal of African and Asian Studies. Vol. 28, 2016. International Journal of African and Asian Studies. 28. Pages 39 – 49.

Nayak, Purusottam (2008), Human Development: Concept and Measurement.
Published in P. Nayak (ed.) Growth and Human Development in North East India, Oxford University Press, New Delhi. Pages 3 - 18.

Neamtu, Daniela and Ciobanu, Oana. (2014). Human Development, Premise For Socio-Economic Development. Global Journal of Commerce and Management Perspective. 3. 32-35.

Noor, Salih O. (2015), From SAPs to PRSPs: The Annals of Neoliberal Ideological Dogmatism in Governance and Development Policy. Critique. Fall 2015. Pages 67 - 104.

Ohiorhenuan, J.F.E. (2011), The future of poverty and development in Africa. Foresight, Vol. 13 No. 3. Pages 7 - 23.

Osabu-Kle, D.T. (2000), The Politics of One-Sided Adjustment in Africa. Journal of Black Studies. 2000;30 (4):515-533.

Oxfam International (2001), Making PRSPs Work: The role of poverty assessments.
Oxfam GB for Oxfam International under ISBN 978-1-84814-492-7.

Oxfam Discussion Papers (2019), The Humanitarian-Development-Peace Nexus. What does it mean for multi-mandated organizations? Oxfam GB for Oxfam International. June 2019.
ISBN 978-1-78748-443-6.

Pan American Health Organization (PAHO), (1999), Humanitarian assistance in disaster situations: A guide for effective aid. Washington, D.C.: PAHO, c1999.
ISBN 92 75 12301 2.

Quibria, M.G. (2002), Growth and Poverty: Lessons from the East Asian Miracle Revisited. ADB Institute Research Paper 33. ADBI Publishing. Tokyo

Qureshi, Sajda (2019), Perspectives on development: why does studying information and communication technology for development (ICT4D) matter?
Information Technology for Development, 25:3. Pages 381 – 389.
DOI: 10.1080/02681102.2019.1658478

Rahman, Raja Abdar; Raja, Muhammad Adil and Ryan, Conor (2020), The Impact of Human Development on Economic Growth: A Panel Data Approach.
SSRN: https://ssrn.com/abstract=3526909
DOI: http://dx.doi.org/10.2139/ssrn.3526909

Ranis, Gustav (2004a), Human Development and Economic Growth.
Available at SSRN: https://ssrn.com/abstract=551662

Ranis, Gustav (2004b), The Evolution of Development Thinking: Theory and Policy.
Available at SSRN: https://ssrn.com/abstract=551645

Ranis, Gustav and Stewart, Frances (2005), Dynamic Links between the Economy and Human Development. DESA Working Paper No. 8. ST/ESA/2005/DWP/8. November 2005.
https://www.un.org/sites/un2.un.org/files/1597341811.4241.pdf

Reisman, Kim (1992), The World Bank And The IMF: At The Forefront Of World Transformation, Fordham Law Review; Volume 60, Issue 6, Article 16. Pages S349 - S394.

Roberts, Les and Hofmann, Charles-Antoine (2004), Assessing the impact of humanitarian assistance in the health sector. Emerging Themes in Epidemiology 2004, 1:3. DOI: 10.1186/1742-7622-1-3.

Rohwerder, B. (2014), The impact of conflict on poverty. GSDRC Helpdesk Research Report 1118. Birmingham, UK: GSDRC, University of Birmingham.

Ruckert, Arne (2006), Towards an Inclusive-Neoliberal Regime of Development: From the Washington to the Post-Washington Consensus.
Labour, Capital and Society 39:1. Pages 36 – 67.

Ruger, J. P. (2005), The changing role of the World Bank in global health.
American journal of public health, 95(1). Pages 60 – 70.
DOI: https://doi.org/10.2105/AJPH.2004.042002

Ryfman, Phillip (2007), Non-governmental organizations: an indispensable player of humanitarian aid. International Review of the Red Cross. Volume 89 Number 865 March 2007. Pages 21 – 45.

Staicu, Gabriel and Barbulescu, Razvan (2017), A Study of the Relationship between Foreign Aid and Human Development in Africa. In "International Development". Edited by Seth Appiah-Opoku.
Available from: www.intechopen.com/chapters/54321

Stewart F. (2002), Root causes of violent conflict in developing countries.
BMJ. 2002 Feb 9;324(7333). Pages 342 - 345. DOI: 10.1136/bmj.324.7333.342.

Stewart, Frances and Wang, Michael (2003), Do PRSPs empower poor countries and disempower the World Bank, or is it the other way round?
QEH Working Papers qehwps108, Queen Elizabeth House, University of Oxford.

Stiglitz, Joseph E. (1998), Towards a New Paradigm for Development: Strategies, Policies, and Processes. Given as the 1998 Prebisch Lecture at UNCTAD,
Geneva October 19, 1998.

Stiglitz, Joseph E. (2003), Democratizing the International Monetary Fund and the World Bank: Governance and Accountability. In "Governance. An International Journal of Policy, Administration, and Institutions". Volume16, Issue1. January 2003.
John Wiley & Sons, Inc. Pages 111-139.

Stiglitz, Joseph E. (2008), Is there a Post-Washington Consensus Consensus? In "The Washington Consensus Reconsidered. Towards a New Global Governance."
Edited by Narcís Serra and Joseph E. Stiglitz. Oxford University Press.
ISBN-13: 9780199534081. Pages 41 – 56.

Stiglitz, Joseph E. (2008b), The Future of Global Governance. In "The Washington Consensus Reconsidered. Towards a New Global Governance." Edited by Narcís Serra and Joseph E. Stiglitz. Oxford University Press.
ISBN-13: 9780199534081. Pages 309 – 323.

Stiglitz, Joseph E. (2020), Measuring What Matters. Scientific American, Volume 323, Issue 2. August 2020. Pages 24-31.

Studer, Meinrad and Fox, Oliver (2005), The Role of Humanitarian and Development Organisations in Relation to the Security Sector in Transition Situations. In "After Intervention: Public Security Management in Post - Conflict Societies - From Intervention to Sustainable Local Ownership. PfP Consortium Working Group "Security Sector Reform". Edited by Anja H. Ebnöther and Philipp H. Fluri.
Vienna and Geneva, August 2005. ISBN: 3-902275-17-0. Pages 385 – 375.

Tamminga, Philip (2011), Sustainability in humanitarian action. Basis of a panel discussion: "Sustainable Humanitarian Action: Bridging relief to development". 31st International Conference of the Red Cross And Red Crescent Geneva, 28 November to 1 December 2011.

Thérien, Jean-Philippe (2004), The Politics of International Development: Towards a New Grand Compromise? EcoLomic Policy and Law, 2004-5.

Thibane, Tankiso A. and Wait, Charles V.R. (2017), During and After the Great Recession: The Role of the International Monetary Fund, the World Bank and the World Trade Organization in Respect of Economic Globalization.
Paper Presented at the Biennial Conference of the Economic Society of South Africa. Grahamstown: Rhodes University, 30 August-1 September 2017.

Thomas, A. (2004), The Study of Development. Paper prepared for DSA Annual Conference, 6 November, Church House, London.

Thomson, Michael; Kentikelenis, Alexander and Stubbs, Thomas (2017), Structural adjustment programmes adversely affect vulnerable populations: a systematic-narrative review of their effect on child and maternal health. Public Health Reviews 38, Article 13. DOI: https://doi.org/10.1186/s40985-017-0059-2.

UNCTAD (2006), The Least Developed Countries Report 2006. United Nations, New York and Geneva.

UNDP (2001), Human Development Report 2001.
Making New Technologies Work for Human Development.
UNHCR (2020), Education in Emergencies coordination. Harnessing humanitarian and development architecture for Education 2030. A report on the Global Partners Project. August 2020.

Voutsa, Maria Eleni and Borovas, George (2015), The role of the Bretton Woods institutions in global economic governance.
Procedia Economics and Finance 19 (2015) 37 – 50.

Voutsa, Maria Eleni; Borovas, George and Fotopoulos, Nikos (2014), The Role of the Bretton Woods institutions in forming and spreading education policies.
Procedia Economics and Finance 9 (2014). Pages 83 – 97.

Weaver, Catherine (2008), Hypocrisy Trap: The World Bank and the Poverty of Reform. Princeton University Press.
[Excerpt: Chaper Six: The Fog Of Development. Pages 176 – 192.
https://www.jstor.org/stable/j.ctt7rv01
Internet – Accessed 10 October 2021]

Wesley, Carlos (1989), Millions die every year in IMF's new Holocaust. EIR Volume 16, Number 5, January 27, 1989. Pages 32 – 34.

Willetts, Juliet; Cheney, Helen and Crawford, Paul (2007), Defining And Refining Effectiveness: Applying Narrative And Dialogue Methods In Aid Monitoring And Evaluation. In "Measuring Effectiveness In Humanitarian And Development Aid: Conceptual Frameworks, Principles And Practice." Edited by Andre M. N. Renzaho. Nova Science Publishers, Inc. ISBN 978-1-60021-959-7. Pages 51 - 68.

Willis, Katie (2011), Theories and Practices of Development. Second edition. Taylor & Francis. London and New York. ISBN 0-203-84418-1.

Wohlwend, Daniela A. (2009), Considering the International Monetary Fund and World Bank: Lending Effectiveness in Sub-Saharan Africa.
In "Topical Review Digest: Human Rights In Sub-Saharan Africa. Human Rights & Human Welfare". Edited by Arianna Nowakowski. Pages 89 – 101.

Wolff, Mark J. (2013), Failure of the International Monetary Fund and World Bank to Achieve Integral Development: A Critical Historical Assessment of Bretton Woods Institutions' Policies, Structures and Governance. Syracuse Journal Of International Law And Commerce: Vol. 41: No. 1, Article 4.

World Bank (2005), Economic Growth in the 1990s: Learning from a Decade of Reform. Washington, DC: World Bank. ISBN-10: 0-8213-6043-4

Wortel, Eva (1993), Humanitarians and their moral stance in war: the underlying values. In Selected Article On International Humanitarian Law. International Review of the Red Cross. Volume 91 Number 876 December 2009. Pages 779 – 802.

Yakubovska, Nataliya (2013), The evolution of development thinking: future of theory and practice. Юридичний вісник. 2. Pages 69 - 73.

You, J.-I. (2002) The Bretton Woods Institutions: Evolution, Reform, and Change. In: Nayyar, D. (Ed.). Governing Globalization.

Yueru, Jin; Duanyi, Liu and Yuhan, Li (2018), Factors That Have Led to the Collapse of the Bretton Woods System. American Journal of Industrial and Business Management, 2018, 8, 2133-2142.

Websites

Oxford Dictionary definitions of *growth*
https://www.oxfordlearnersdictionaries.com/definition/english/growth?q=growth
Internet – Accessed 05 May 2021

Oxford Dictionary definitions of *development*
https://www.oxfordlearnersdictionaries.com/definition/english/development?q=development
Internet – Accessed 05 May 2021

World Commission on Environment and Development (WCED), 1987 Report of the World Commission on Environment and Development: Our Common Future
https://sustainabledevelopment.un.org/content/documents/5987our-common-future.pdf
Internet – Accessed 05 May 2021

SOAS (Unknown a), Understanding Sustainable Development.
Unit 1 The Challenge of Sustainable Development
https://www.soas.ac.uk/cedep-demos/000_P501_USD_K3736-Demo/unit1/page_12.htm
Internet – Accessed 20 May 2021

SOAS (Unknown b), Climate Change and Development
Unit 1 Climate Change and Development Challenges
https://www.soas.ac.uk/cedep-demos/000_P524_CCD_K3736-Demo/unit1/page_13.htm#
Internet – Accessed 20 May 2021

Tutor2u (2021), Key Gap Indicators of Development
https://www.tutor2u.net/geography/reference/the-8-key-gap-indicators-of-development
Internet – Accessed 20 May 2021

BBC (2021), Contrasts in development between different countries
https://www.bbc.co.uk/bitesize/guides/z838xsg/revision/2
Internet – Accessed 20 May 2021

Study Rocket (Unknown),
Measures of Development
https://studyrocket.co.uk/revision/a-level-economics-a-edexcel/a-global-perspective/measures-of-development
Internet – Accessed 20 May 2021

Heikkinen, Risto (2021), Measuring development: policies and indicators
https://www.theseus.fi/bitstream/handle/10024/30671/Heikkinen%20Risto.pdf?sequence=2
Internet – Accessed 20 May 2021

Royal Geographical Society (RGS) (Unknown), Development Indicators
https://www.rgs.org/CMSPages/GetFile.aspx?nodeguid=0e147402-c274-4fdd-8bcb-fd614d85f0eb&lang=en-GB
Internet – Accessed 20 May 2021

United Nations Department of Economic and Social Affairs (Unknown), Sustainable Development 17 Goals
https://sdgs.un.org/goals
Internet – Accessed 21 May 2021

The World Bank Group (2021a), The World Bank
https://www.worldbank.org/en/home
Internet – Accessed 22 May 2021

The World Bank Group (2021b), The World Bank Group and the International Monetary Fund (IMF). What is the difference between the World Bank Group and the IMF?
https://www.worldbank.org/en/about/history/the-world-bank-group-and-the-imf#:~:text=What%20is%20the%20difference%20between%20the%20World%20Bank%20Group%20and%20the%20IMF%3F&text=The%20World%20Bank%20Group%20works,monitor%20of%20the%20world's%20currencies.
Internet – Accessed 22 May 2021

The World Bank Group (2021c), WDR Reports
https://www.worldbank.org/en/publication/wdr/wdr-archive
Internet – Accessed 22 May 2021

Bretton Woods Project (2019), What are the Bretton Woods Institutions?
https://www.brettonwoodsproject.org/2019/01/art-320747/#:~:text=The%20Bretton%20Woods%20Institutions%20are,to%20promote%20international%20economic%20cooperation
Internet – Accessed 22 May 2021

The World Bank Group and the International Monetary Fund (IMF). What is the difference between the World Bank Group and the IMF?
https://www.worldbank.org/en/about/history/the-world-bank-group-and-the-imf#:~:text=What%20is%20the%20difference%20between%20the%20World%20Bank%20Group%20and%20the%20IMF%3F&text=The%20World%20Bank%20Group%20works,monitor%20of%20the%20world's%20currencies.
Internet – Accessed 22 May 2021

International Monetary Fund (2021), World Economic Outlook Reports
https://www.imf.org/en/Publications/WEO
Internet – Accessed 22 May 2021

Saldanha, Jean; Perera, Mark; Romero, Maria Jose and Brunswijck, Gino (2019),
The Bretton Woods Institutions, 75 years on: reform or risk irrelevance.
https://www.eurodad.org/75_years_bretton_woods_institutions
Internet – Accessed 22 May 2021

Romero, María José (2020), Bretton Woods Institutions challenged by the outbreak of Covid-19
https://study.soas.ac.uk/bretton-woods-institutions-challenged-by-the-outbreak-of-covid-19/
Internet – Accessed 24 May 2021

Serrate, José Siaba (2020), Assessing the 'new Bretton Woods' moment
https://www.orfonline.org/expert-speak/assessing-new-bretton-woods-moment/
Internet – Accessed 24 May 2021

Brundtland, Gro Harlem (2020), A new 'Bretton Woods' moment is key to building back better after COVID-19
https://theelders.org/news/new-bretton-woods-moment-key-building-back-better-after-covid-19
Internet – Accessed 24 May 2021

Degnarain, Nishan (2020), The Great Coronavirus Reset: Five New Bretton Woods Institutions For 21st Century's Exponential Challenges
https://www.forbes.com/sites/nishandegnarain/2020/03/24/the-great-coronavirus-reset-five-new-bretton-woods-institutions-for-21st-centurys-exponential-challenges/?sh=290263635ca1
Internet – Accessed 24 May 2021

Arcelli, Angelo Federico and Tria, Giovanni (2021), Imagining a Post-COVID-19 Scenario for a Renewed Bretton Woods Agreement
https://www.cigionline.org/articles/imagining-post-covid-19-scenario-renewed-bretton-woods-agreement/
Internet – Accessed 24 May 2021

Chowdhury, Anis and Sundaram, Jomo Kwame (2019); Bretton Woods Institutions: From Solution to Problem
http://www.ipsnews.net/2019/07/bretton-woods-institutions-solution-problem/
Internet – Accessed 25 May 2021

Parkinson, Martin (2014), Are the Bretton Woods Institutions Still Relevant for the Emerging Market Economies? At Reinventing Bretton Woods Conference 11 April, Washington DC.
https://treasury.gov.au/sites/default/files/2019-03/Bretton Woods_Speech.pdf
Internet – Accessed 25 May 2021

Allegret, J.P. and Dulbecco, P. (2004), The Institutional Failures of Bretton Woods Institutions Conditionality.
Annual Meeting of the European Public Choice Society Berlin, April 15-18, 2004.
https://www.diw.de/documents/dokumentenarchiv/17/41580/Paper-064.pdf
Internet – Accessed 25 May 2021

Stein H. (2010) Crises and the Bretton Woods Institutions and the Crises of the Bretton Woods Institutions. Paper Prepared for the Conference Impacts, Responses & Initial Lessons of the Financial Crisis for Low Income Countries Danish Institute for International Studies Copenhagen 14, 15 October 2010
https://www.diis.dk/files/media/publications/import/stein.howard.pdf
Internet – Accessed 25 May 2021

Williamson, John (2004), A Short History of the Washington Consensus
Paper commissioned by Fundación CIDOB for a conference "From the Washington Consensus towards a new Global Governance," Barcelona, September 24–25, 2004.
https://www.piie.com/publications/papers/williamson0904-2.pdf
Internet – Accessed 25 May 2021

Frieden, Jeffry (2017), The political economy of the Bretton Woods Agreements
https://scholar.harvard.edu/files/jfrieden/files/frieden_brettonwoods_dec2017.pdf
Internet – Accessed 25 May 2021

Kwagyang, Garba Umaru; Ghide, Hamman Buba and Haruna, Abdulrashid Lawan (2015), Bretton Woods Institutions: Their Evolution and Impacts on the Field of International Economic Law. Journal of Law, Policy and Globalization. ISSN 2224-3240 (Paper) ISSN 2224-3259 (Online) Vol.35, 2015
https://core.ac.uk/download/pdf/234650088.pdf
Internet – Accessed 25 May 2021

UN OCHA (2012); What are Humanitarian Principles?
https://www.unocha.org/sites/dms/Documents/OOM-humanitarianprinciples_eng_June12.pdf
Internet – Accessed 27 May 2021

Sphere Association (2018), The Humanitarian Charter. Common principles, rights and duties.
https://handbook.spherestandards.org/en/sphere/#ch003_001
Internet – Accessed 27 May 2021

Malin, Lance J (2013), The Logical Framework Approach: Is this the most appropriate instrument for managing the elimination of the threat posed by landmines and Explosive Remnants of War in South Sudan?
https://kaluinstitute.org/wp-content/uploads/attachments/LanceMalin/LFA-ManagingLandmines&ERW-23Nov13.pdf
Internet – Accessed 27 May 2021

Mary B. Anderson (2000), Options For Aid in Conflict Lessons from Field Experience.
https://www.cdacollaborative.org/wp-content/uploads/2016/01/Options-for-Aid-in-Conflict-Lessons-from-Field-Experience.pdf
Internet – Accessed 31 May 2021

Mary B. Anderson (1999), "Indications" for Assessing Aid's Impacts on Conflict
https://www.cdacollaborative.org/wp-content/uploads/2016/02/Indications-for-Assessing-Aids-Impacts-on-Conflict.pdf
Internet – Accessed 31 May 2021

OHCHR (2011), Declaration on the Right to Development
https://www.ohchr.org/Documents/Issues/Development/RTD_booklet_en.pdf
Internet – Accessed 31 May 2021

United Nations Development Programme (UNDP) (Unknown),
Human Development Index (HDI)
http://hdr.undp.org/en/content/human-development-index-hdi
Internet – Accessed 04 June 2021

McGill University School of Computer Science (2021), Margin of error
https://www.cs.mcgill.ca/~rwest/wikispeedia/wpcd/wp/m/Margin_of_error.htm
Internet – Accessed 04 June 2021

Good Humanitarian Donorship (GHD) (2016), Principles And Good Practice Of Humanitarian Donorship
https://www.ghdinitiative.org/ghd/gns/principles-good-practice-of-ghd/principles-good-practice-ghd.html
Internet – Accessed 06 June 2021

Phillips, Keri (2013), The history of foreign aid
https://reliefweb.int/report/world/history-foreign-aid
Internet – Accessed 06 June 2021

AECID and DARA (Unknown), Now Or Never. Making Humanitarian Aid More Effective
http://resources.daraint.org/hardtalk/aid_effectiveness.pdf
Internet – Accessed 07 June 2021

Balendran, Kailash (2019), The humanitarian and development sectors need to collaborate, but how can we make it work?
https://www.opml.co.uk/blog/the-humanitarian-and-development-sectors-need-to-collaborate-but-how-can-we-make-it-work
Internet – Accessed 07 June 2021

Kopinak, Janice K. (2013), Humanitarian Aid: Are Effectiveness and Sustainability Impossible Dreams?
https://sites.tufts.edu/jha/archives/1935
Internet – Accessed 07 June 2021

Society for International Development (SID), (2021), What is Development?
https://sid-israel.org/en/what-is-development/
Internet – Accessed 11 June 2021

Barder, Owen (2012), What Is Development?
https://www.cgdev.org/blog/what-development
Internet – Accessed 11 June 2021

Elliott, Larry (2016), The World Bank and the IMF won't admit their policies are the problem.
https://www.theguardian.com/business/2016/oct/09/the-world-bank-and-the-imf-wont-admit-their-policies-are-the-problem
Internet – Accessed 11 June 2021

Lombardi, Domenico and Momani, Bessma (2010), Explaining IMF and World Bank Relationship. Prepared for: The Political Economy of International Organizations (PEIO). January 28 – 30, 2010, Washington DC, Georgetown University
https://www.peio.me/wp-content/uploads/2014/04/Conf3_Lombardi-Momani-26.01.10.pdf
Internet – Accessed 11 June 2021

Chowdhury, Anis and Sundaram, Jomo Kwame (2019), Bretton Woods Institutions: From Solution to Problem.
http://www.ipsnews.net/2019/07/bretton-woods-institutions-solution-problem/
Internet – Accessed 11 June 2021

Colgan, Ann-Louise (2002), Hazardous to Health: The World Bank and IMF in Africa
https://www.pambazuka.org/governance/hazardous-health-world-bank-and-imf-africa
Internet – Accessed 12 June 2021

Driscoll, David D. (1996), The IMF and the World Bank. How Do They Differ?
https://www.imf.org/external/pubs/ft/exrp/differ/differ.htm
Internet – Accessed 12 June 2021

Lahdenperä, Jori and Humayoun, Shehzad (2010), The International Monetary Fund (IMF) and World Bank Structural Adjustment Programs. Review study of adjustment-aid theory.
https://www.diva-portal.org/smash/get/diva2:327908/FULLTEXT01.pdf
Internet – Accessed 13 June 2021

Nyikal, Harold (2005), Neo-Colonialism In Africa: The Economic Crisis In Africa And The Propagation Of The Status Quo By The World Bank/IMF And WTO.
https://web.stanford.edu/class/e297a/Neo-Colonialism%20in%20Africa.pdf
Internet – Accessed 13 June 2021

Githua, Doris Wangui (2011), The Impact Of International Monetary Fund (Imf) And The World Bank Structural Adjustment Programmes In Developing Countries. Case Study Of Kenya
http://erepository.uonbi.ac.ke/bitstream/handle/11295/60212/Githua_The%20impact%20%20of%20International%20Monetary%20Fund%20(IMF)%20and%20the%20World%20Bank%20structural%20adjustment%20programmes.pdf?sequence=3
Internet – Accessed 13 June 2021

Odutayo, Aramide (2015), Conditional Development: Ghana Crippled by Structural Adjustment Programmes. E-International Relations.
https://www.e-ir.info/pdf/54420
Internet – Accessed 14 June 2021

Toussaint, Eric (2020), The World Bank, the IMF and the respect of human rights
https://www.cadtm.org/The-World-Bank-the-IMF-and-the-respect-of-human-rights
Internet – Accessed 14 June 2021

Buckland, Jerry (1998), From Relief and Development to Assisted Self-Reliance: Nongovernmental Organizations in Bangladesh
https://sites.tufts.edu/jha/archives/144
Internet – Accessed 16 June 2021

Hilhorst, D.J.M. (2007), Saving lives or saving societies? Realities of relief and reconstruction.
https://edepot.wur.nl/231139
Internet – Accessed 16 June 2021

Rama, Martina (2017), Linking Relief, Rehabilitation and Development (LRRD):
Examples and Lessons learned for the WASH sector.
https://www.pseau.org/outils/ouvrages/hydroconseil_wedc_linking_relief_rehabilitation_and_development_lrrd_examples_and_lessons_learned_for_the_wash_sector_2017.pdf
Internet – Accessed 19 June 2021

Humanitarian Leadership Academy, HLA (2019), The Future of Skills in the Humanitarian Sector
https://www.humanitarianleadershipacademy.org/wp-content/uploads/2019/10/Future-of-Skills-in-the-Humanitarian-Sector-Report_4MB.pdf
Internet – Accessed 20 June 2021

Balendran, Kailash (2019), The humanitarian and development sectors need to collaborate, but how can we make it work?
https://www.opml.co.uk/blog/the-humanitarian-and-development-sectors-need-to-collaborate-but-how-can-we-make-it-work
Internet – Accessed 20 June 2021

Irish Times (2002), IMF empire strikes back at World Bank's 'beautiful mind' Stiglitz
https://www.irishtimes.com/business/imf-empire-strikes-back-at-world-bank-s-beautiful-mind-stiglitz-1.1088085
Internet – Accessed 21 June 2021

Cassidy, John (2002), Master of Disaster.
A leading economist says the protesters have a point about the I.M.F
https://www.newyorker.com/magazine/2002/07/15/master-of-disaster
Internet – Accessed 21 June 2021

OECD (2017), Humanitarian Development Coherence
https://www.oecd.org/development/humanitarian-donors/docs/COHERENCE-OECD-Guideline.pdf
Internet – Accessed 23 June 2021

Ngirumpatse, Pauline (2019), Tackling Development Effectiveness: A spectrum of unfinished business(es).
http://southernvoice.org/tackling-development-effectiveness-a-spectrum-of-unfinished-businesses/
Internet – Accessed 23 June 2021

Prolog Consult (2007), Evaluation Of Humanitarian Aid By And For NGOs. A guide with ideas to consider when designing your own evaluation activities.
https://www.alnap.org/system/files/content/resource/files/main/humanitarian-guide.pdf
Internet – Accessed 23 June 2021

ODI (2018), Measuring the hard to measure in development
https://odi.org/en/events/measuring-the-hard-to-measure-in-development/
Internet – Accessed 25 June 2021

Ramalingam, Ben; Mitchell, John; Borton, John and Smart, Kristin (2014);
Counting what counts: performance and effectiveness in the humanitarian sector.
https://www.humanitarianlibrary.org/sites/default/files/2014/02/8rhach1.pdf
Internet – Accessed 25 June 2021

STCI, UNPD (2013), Measuring the effectiveness of development cooperation at the local level – Ecuador.
https://www.local2030.org/library/61/Measuring-the-effectiveness-of-development-cooperation-at-the-local-level-%E2%80%93-Ecuador.pdf
Internet – Accessed 25 June 2021

Watson, Cathy (2008), Impact Assessment of Humanitarian Response: A review of the literature.
https://www.alnap.org/system/files/content/resource/files/main/impact-10-07-08.pdf
Internet – Accessed 25 June 2021

Dagne, Seblewengel Debebe (2014), Impact of Development and Humanitarian Aid on Economic Growth of Developing Countries.
https://edepot.wur.nl/302731
Internet – Accessed 27 June 2021

CATO Institute (Unknown), The Human Freedom Index
https://www.cato.org/human-freedom-index/2020
Internet – Accessed 02 July 2021

The Heritage Foundation (Unknown), The Index of Economic Freedom
https://www.heritage.org/index/
Internet – Accessed 02 July 2021

Driscoll, Ruth and Christiansen, Karin (2004), The PRSP Approach. A basic guide for CARE International. Overseas Development Institute, London.
https://odi.org/en/publications/the-prsp-approach-a-basic-guide-for-care-international/
Internet – Accessed 05 July 2021

Stiglitz, Joseph E. (2001), To a Third Way Consensus
https://www.project-syndicate.org/commentary/to-a-third-way-consensus
Internet – Accessed 07 July 2021

Daste, Héloïse (2015), The role of the Bretton Woods institutions in development cooperation.
https://www.academia.edu/28644417/The_role_of_the_Bretton_Woods_institutions_in_development_cooperation
Internet – Accessed 15 July 2021

UN/DESA (2017), UN/DESA Policy Brief #52: The Marshall Plan, IMF and First UN Development Decade in the Golden Age of Capitalism: lessons for our time.
https://www.un.org/development/desa/dpad/publication/policy-brief-52-the-marshall-plan-imf-and-first-un-development-decade-in-the-golden-age-of-capitalism-lessons-for-our-time/
Internet – Accessed 16 July 2021

IMF (2021), About the IMF
https://www.imf.org/en/About
Internet – Accessed 19 July 2021

Williamson, John (2004), The Washington Consensus as Policy Prescription for Development
https://www.piie.com/commentary/speeches-papers/washington-consensus-policy-prescription-development
https://www.piie.com/sites/default/files/publications/papers/williamson0204.pdf
Internet – Accessed 25 July 2021

United Nations Development Programme (UNDP) (2020), Human Development Index (HDI)
http://hdr.undp.org/sites/default/files/hdr2020.pdf
Internet – Accessed 25 July 2021

Ban, Ki-Moon (2016), One humanity: shared responsibility. Report of the Secretary-General for the World Humanitarian Summit. 2 February 2016.
https://reliefweb.int/sites/reliefweb.int/files/resources/Secretary-General%27s%20Report%20for%20WHS%202016%20%28Advance%20Unedited%20Draft%29.pdf
Internet – Accessed 27 July 2021

World Economic Forum Global Agenda Council on Humanitarian Assistance (2009), A New Business Model for Humanitarian Assistance? A challenge paper.
https://www.international-alert.org/sites/default/files/publications/A_new_business_model_for_humanitarian_assistance_WEF_Nov09.pdf
Internet – Accessed 29 July 2021

OHCHR (1986), Declaration on the Right to Development
https://www.ohchr.org/en/professionalinterest/pages/righttodevelopment.aspx#:~:text=1.,freedoms%20can%20be%20fully%20realized.
Internet – Accessed 31 July 2021

Linking Humanitarian Aid and Development Aid: A Lively Discussion With Julia Steets and Other Experts. January 16, 2017
JICA Ogata Sadako Research Institute for Peace and Development
(JICA Ogata Research Institute)
https://www.jica.go.jp/jica-ri/news/topics/20161212_01.html
Internet – Accessed 02 August 2021

World Humanitarian Summit (2016), High-Level Panel on Humanitarian Financing Report to the Secretary-General. Too important to fail—addressing the humanitarian financing gap
https://reliefweb.int/report/world/high-level-panel-humanitarian-financing-report-secretary-general-too-important-fail
Internet – Accessed 06 August 2021

Bruce-Lockhart, Anna (2016), What do we mean by 'governance'?
https://www.weforum.org/agenda/2016/02/what-is-governance-and-why-does-it-matter/
Internet – Accessed 06 August 2021

Learning for Sustainability, LFS (2021), Governance and good governance
https://learningforsustainability.net/good-governance/
Internet – Accessed 06 August 2021

Fengler, Wolfgang and Kharas, Homi (2016), Overview: Delivering Aid Differently
https://www.brookings.edu/wp-content/uploads/2016/07/deliveringaiddifferently_chapter.pdf
Internet – Accessed 06 August 2021

El-Tom, Abdullahi (1994), Mugging the poor: the Bretton Woods institutions and the pursuit of African development.
Institute for African Alternatives (IFAA).
https://mural.maynoothuniversity.ie/1382/1/IFAA.pdf
Internet – Accessed 08 August 2021

Swanson, Ana (2015), Why trying to help poor countries might actually hurt them
https://www.washingtonpost.com/news/wonk/wp/2015/10/13/why-trying-to-help-poor-countries-might-actually-hurt-them/
Internet – Accessed 08 August 2021

The World Bank (2020), COVID-19 to Add as Many as 150 Million Extreme Poor by 2021
https://www.worldbank.org/en/news/press-release/2020/10/07/covid-19-to-add-as-many-as-150-million-extreme-poor-by-2021
Internet – Accessed 16 August 2021

Chambers, Robert (2012), Participation for Development: Why is this a good time to be alive?
https://participationpower.wordpress.com/2013/01/07/participation-for-development-why-is-this-a-good-time-to-be-alive/
Internet – Accessed 16 August 2021

UNDP (2020), The 2020 Human Development Report The next frontier - Human development and the Anthropocene.
http://hdr.undp.org/sites/default/files/hdr2020.pdf
Internet – Accessed 18 August 2021

Birdsall, Nancy (2019), The World Bank Needs to Join the 21st Century
https://foreignpolicy.com/2019/01/16/the-world-bank-needs-to-join-the-21st-century/
Internet – Accessed 20 August 2021

Heckman, James J. (2016), Human Development is Economic Development. Rancho Santa Fe San Diego, California February 25th, 2016.
https://heckmanequation.org/www/assets/2017/01/F_San-Diego-JB-HO_SLIDES_2016-02-23b_jbb.pdf
Internet – Accessed 27 August 2021

Karpowicz, Katarzyna (2008), Economic Growth and Development: Is High GDP Enough?
https://www.e-ir.info/2008/02/23/economic-growth-and-development-is-high-gdp-enough/
Internet – Accessed 29 August 2021

Alonso, Lucas J. M. Alonso (2015), Economic Growth, Human Development and Global Socio Economic Imbalances: How do you think the progress of a country can be measured?
https://www.ucm.es/emui/economic-growth-human-development-and-global-socio-economic-imbalances
Internet – Accessed 29 August 2021

Ibrahim, Habiba A. (2017), NGOs And Development Work In Developing Countries:
A Critical Review
https://american-jiras.com/Ibrahim-ManuscriptRef.2-ajira100517.pdf
Internet – Accessed 30 August 2021

Matthewman, Joshua (2012), The Bretton Woods Institutions and Development Partnerships
https://www.e-ir.info/pdf/17440
Internet – Accessed 12 October 2021

United Nations (2003), Monterrey Consensus of the International Conference on Financing for Development
https://www.un.org/en/events/pastevents/pdfs/MonterreyConsensus.pdf
Internet – Accessed 13 October 2021

Overseas Development Institute (1993), Does The IMF Really Help Developing Countries? Briefing Paper April 1993. Overseas Development Institute 1993.
ISSN 0140-8682.
https://cdn.odi.org/media/documents/6784.pdf
Internet – Accessed 14 October 2021

Masters, Jonathan and Chatzky, Andrew (2019), The World Bank Group's Role in Global Development.
https://www.cfr.org/backgrounder/world-bank-groups-role-global-development
Internet – Accessed 14 October 2021

Cepeda, Ricardo David Ruiz (2021), Have the Bretton Woods Financial Institutions failed the Global South?
https://www.linkedin.com/pulse/have-bretton-woods-financial-institutions-failed-ruiz-cepeda?trk=public_profile_article_view
Internet – Accessed 15 October 2021

Romero, Maria Jose (2020), If not now, then when? The Bretton Woods Institutions' response to Covid-19
https://study.soas.ac.uk/bretton-woods-world-bank-group-covid-19/
Internet – Accessed 15 October 2021

Romero, Maria Jose; Perera, Mark; Brunswijck, Gino and Saldanha, Jean (2019),
The Bretton Woods Institutions, 75 years on: reform or risk irrelevance.
https://www.eurodad.org/75_years_bretton_woods_institutions
Internet – Accessed 15 October 2021

Toussaint, Eric (2020b), The World Bank and the IMF in Indonesia: an emblematic interference
https://www.cadtm.org/spip.php?page=imprimer&id_article=10860
Internet – Accessed 16 October 2021

APPENDICES

Appendix A: Online survey hosted on SurveyMonkey.com

https://surveymonkey.com/r/RXZ89CW

Appendix B: 17 Sustainable Development Goals (SDGs)

Source: https://sdgs.un.org/goals

Internet – Accessed 25 May 2021

Appendix C: Correlation Coefficient – Questions 1 and 4

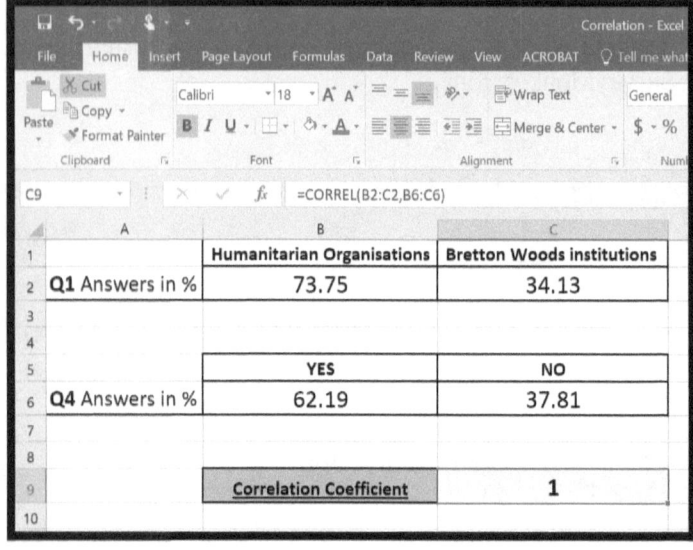

Appendix D: Governance

Good governance always involves a range of different elements.
Source: Learning for Sustainability

Source: Australian National Audit Office
Cited by Bruce-Lockhart (2016)

www.ingramcontent.com/pod-product-compliance
Lightning Source LLC
Chambersburg PA
CBHW031419210526
45464CB00005B/1953